What do the Religions say about Each Other?

CHRISTIAN ATTITUDES TOWARDS ISLAM

ISLAMIC ATTITUDES TOWARDS CHRISTIANITY

Compiled by William Stoddart

For information, address:
Sophia Perennis,
P.O. Box 151011
San Rafael, CA 94915
sophiaperennis.com

Library of Congress Cataloging-in-Publication Data

What do the religions say about each other? : Christian attitudes
towards Islam, Islamic attitudes towards Christianity / compiled by
William Stoddart. – 1st ed.
p. cm.
Includes bibliographical references.
ISBN 978-1-59731-089-5 (pbk. : alk. paper)
1. Islam–Relations–Christianity. 2. Christianity and other religions-
-Islam. 3. Religious tolerance–Islam. 4. Religious tolerance–
Christianity. 5. Religions–Relations. I. Stoddart, William.
BP172.W5 2008
261.2'7–dc22
2008034371

Other Books by the Same Author

Remembering in a World of Forgetting: Thoughts on Tradition and Postmodernism
(World Wisdom Books, Bloomington, Indiana, 2008)

Invincible Wisdom: Quotations from the Scriptures, Saints, and Sages of All Times and Places
(Sophia Perennis, Petaluma, California, 2008)

Hinduism and its Spiritual Masters
(first edition, under the title **Outline of Hinduism**: Foundation for Traditional Studies, Oakton, Virginia, 1993; second edition: Fons Vitae, Louisville, Kentucky, 2007)

Outline of Buddhism
(Foundation for Traditional Studies, Oakton, Virginia, 1998)

Sufism: The Mystical Doctrines and Methods of Islam
(first edition, 1976; latest reprint: Paragon House, Saint Paul, Minnesota, 1985)

CONTENTS

ISLAMIC ATTITUDES TOWARDS CHRISTIANITY

The Sufis

Sultans and Saints

Historians

ILLUSTRATIONS

INDEX

INTRODUCTION

(1) Attitudes

The dreadful events and developments of the last few years have caused the Western public to ask, more or less for the first time: what kind of religion is Islam? Those good people who seek conciliation reply that Islam is "a religion of peace". Well, yes, and so is every other religion, although we must not forget that Christ said: "I came not to bring peace but a sword" — and that a principle analogous to this is also present in every religion.

Much more importantly, every religion claims to be, first and foremost, "a religion of truth". In the words of Christ, it is truth that "sets you free". Thus every religion makes the dual claim to be a vehicle of truth, and a provider of a means of salvation. Were it not so, it would not be a religion, but a man-made ideology, with no ability to save anyone. Truth and a means of salvation are the defining characteristics of a religion.

Christianity should be well known to people born and raised in the Western world — although one can no longer take this for granted. As for Islam, it is characterized by what are called "the five pillars". These are: faith, prayer, fasting, almsgiving, and pilgrimage. Faith (*îmân*) that "there is no god but God"; prayer (*salât*) five times a day; fasting (*saum*) during the holy month of Ramadan; almsgiving (*zakât*) "to the poor, the widows, and the orphans"; and pilgrimage (*hajj*) — once in a life-time, if it is possible — to the Abrahamic "black stone" in the Kaaba in Mecca.

When we in the West seek to determine what our attitude towards Islam should be, we cannot do better than carefully ponder the declarations and attitudes of the Scriptures and the spokesmen (learned and humble, ancient and modern) of both religions on the question of their mutual relationship. *Mutatis mutandis*, Muslim believers would be wise to do the same. Only this can provide us with the fundamental knowledge that is indispensable for an understanding in depth.

The examples here presented have been culled only from the traditional or pre-modern form of the religion or denomination concerned. The reason for this is that modern forms of religion — which are now ubiquitous — are subjective, arbitrary, and fluctuating, and lacking in the authority and permanence that are the hallmark of true religion.

The aim of this compilation is to put some of these traditional attitudes and declarations of Christianity regarding Islam, and of Islam regarding Christianity, at the disposal of contemporary people of goodwill.

(2) The Importance of Orthodoxy

The meaning of the term "orthodoxy" has been almost completely effaced from people's minds. More often than not, orthodoxy is considered to be simply a form of intolerance: one group of people attempting to impose their views on others. In this connection, however, it is useful to recall the first item on the "Eightfold Path" of Buddhism: this is "right views" or "right thinking". It is obvious why "right thinking" should enjoy pride of place, for, both logically and practically, it is prior to "right doing". And what is the English word (derived from Greek) that signifies "right thinking"? None other than "orthodoxy".

To take the matter further: $2 + 2 = 4$ is orthodox; $2 + 2 = 5$ is unorthodox. Rather simple — but it also works the same way at much loftier levels. Another way of looking at it is this: even in the circumstances of today, many people still preserve the notion of "moral purity", and lay high value on it. Orthodoxy is "intellectual purity", and as such is an indispensable prelude to grace. Seen in this way — and far from "telling others what to believe" — orthodoxy is no more than a reference to the primacy and priority of truth. Orthodoxy, indeed, is the principle of truth that runs through the myths, symbols, and dogmas which are the very language of revelation.

Like morality, orthodoxy may be either universal (conformity to truth as such) or specific (conformity to the forms of a given religion). It is universal when it declares that God is uncreated, or that God is absolute and infinite. It is specific when it declares that God is Trinitarian (Christianity), or that God takes the triple form of Brahmâ, Vishnu, and Shiva (Hinduism).

Departure from orthodoxy is heresy: either intrinsic (for example, atheism or deism), or extrinsic (for example, an adherent of a Semitic religion rejecting the divinities of the Hindu or Greek pantheons).

Orthodoxy is normal, heresy abnormal. This permits the use of a medical metaphor: the study of the various traditional orthodoxies is the affair of the religious physiologist, whereas the study of heresies (were it worthwhile) is the affair of the religious pathologist.

The English Catholic philosopher Bernard Kelly (1907-1958) knew that the encounter of the world religions was inevitable and, given the special needs of our time, he saw that this had a positive side. His wish was that this encounter might be, not destructive, but for "the greater glory of God"; in other words, not for the loss of souls, but for their salvation. As if foreseeing the modern chaos, his first principle in this domain was that of the overriding need for *orthodoxy* — not only on the part of Christianity, but also on the part of the non-Christian religions which, in both East and West, were being usurped by secularism on the one hand and deformed by denominationalism and/or "fundamentalism" on the other. What was the use, he asked, of comparing, say, Mormonism with Bahai'ism, a Teilhard de Chardin with an Aurobindo, a trendy Jesuit with a "fundamentalist" *ayatollah*. Here is how Kelly put it:

> Confusion is inevitable whenever cultures based on profoundly different spiritual traditions intermingle without rigid safeguards to preserve their purity. The crusader with the cross emblazoned on his breast, the loincloth and spindle of Mahatma Gandhi when he visited Europe, are images of the kind of precaution that is reasonable when traveling in a spiritually alien territory. The modern traveler in his impeccable business suit and necktie is safeguarded by that costume against any lack of seriousness in discussing

finance. Of more important safeguards he knows nothing. The complete secularism of the modern Western world, wherever its influence has spread, has opened the floodgates to a confusion which sweeps away the contours of the spirit. Traditional norms provide the criteria of culture and civilization. Traditional orthodoxy is thus the prerequisite of any discourse at all between the Traditions themselves.[1]

(3) The Downward Cycle

The Hindus say that a complete cycle of time (a *Mahâyuga*) consists of four *Yugas*. These correspond to the Greek concept of the Four Ages: Golden, Silver, Bronze, and Iron. The Hindu name for the Iron Age is *Kali-Yuga*, which literally means "Dark Age", and Hindus aver, not only that we are in the Kali-Yuga, but that we are now in the *last phase* of the Kali-Yuga. Anyone who is sensitive to the colossal moral and social decline in these last few decades will not question the plausibility of this notion. All the more so since Christian (and Islamic) doctrine regarding the "end times" is almost identical to this concept of the "last phase" of the Kali-Yuga.

No one knows exactly when the Kali-Yuga began, but it certainly includes the whole of what is called the "historical period" of approximately 3,000 years. Significantly, it has, from the beginning, been marked by the presence of evil. For example, already many centuries ago, there was the expulsion of Buddhism from Hindu India, which involved horrendous cruelty; there was the entry of the Muslim armies into India, which, at the beginning at least, involved massacres and temple destruction; there was the unending warring in Buddhist Tibet and Buddhist Japan; and there were the pillage, plunder, and rapine of the Crusades, which afflicted chiefly defenseless non-Catholic Christians and Jewish *stetl* which crusaders encountered on their way to the Holy Land — where the Muslims could be relied on to defend themselves. Some

[1]*Dominican Studies* (London), volume 7, 1954, p. 2.

centuries later there was the subjugation and humiliation of the nomadic Plains Indians in North America by Protestants, and the violent suppression of Indians in Central and South America by Catholics.

During the Kali-Yuga, there has been a succession of downward falls or revolutions, each of which ushered in a new, and worse,[2] phase. A decisive fall was the 15th-century Renaissance, which, both intellectually and artistically, put an end to the Middle Ages (already two centuries past their zenith) along with integral Christian civilization ("the age of the cathedrals", "the age of faith"). Since then, there has been a succession of analogous falls: following upon the 17th-century monstrosity of Baroque art,[3] there came the 18th-century "Enlightenment" (epitomized by Voltaire, Rousseau, and the *encyclopédistes*) and the ensuing French Revolution; next came the Industrial Revolution; and then, in the 19th and 20th centuries, came the nefarious quintet: Darwin, Marx, Freud, Jung,[4] and Teilhard de Chardin. Today the influence of these five demons can be seen and felt everywhere around us, that of Teilhard de Chardin being particularly manifest in the Vatican II Council of 1962-65. This Council coincides nicely with the "hippie revolution" of the 1960s. With this last fall, anything recognizable as "morality" began to vanish

---

[2] The Prophet Mohammed said: "No time cometh upon you but is followed by a worse."

[3] Lest this judgement seem too peremptory, let me explain: Baroque painting, architecture, and statuary — in contrast with the Romanesque and Gothic styles of the Middle Ages — indicate only too clearly that the ancient science of symbolism had been lost. In Baroque art, there is a total absence of depth, subtlety, and any awareness of the invisible world of archetypes. Unlike Medieval art, Baroque art is surface, not depth.

[4] Jung is generally regarded as an angel of light. His fatal flaw goes undetected. Jung completely fails to distinguish between soul and Spirit (Eckhart's *Intellectus*), which in practice amounts to the "abolition" of Spirit. At one stroke, he abolishes the capacity for objectivity and, by the same token, for spirituality. The chaos and damage resulting from this anti-Platonic act of blindness are incalculable. We are left stranded in a satanic kingdom where everything (truth, morality, art) is relative.

from the public domain; morality was replaced by "political correctness". Having mentioned the five main demons, one must also mention some of the leading destroyers in the fields of art, architecture, music, and literature, such as, Picasso, Le Corbusier, Schoenberg, James Joyce, and a legion of others.

A particularly characteristic aspect of the Kali-Yuga — and especially of its "last phase" — is, not simply the frequency and atrociousness of violence and warfare, but above all the fact that this warfare most often takes the form of inter-religious conflict.

Against all evidence, the secular humanist maintains that, through "science" and "reason",[5] religion will eventually wither away. This is far from being the case: religion, belief in God, is inscribed deep in the heart of man; it cannot be extinguished. Nevertheless, it is not hard to see that religion also has a negative side, in that all of the great world religions are anchored in immense religious collectivities which, to say the least, are subject to constantly accelerating "change and decay": these collectivities and their self-appointed leaders exploit religion, distort religion, and transform it into a superficial and competitive "denominationalism". Though the eternal message present in the heart of each religion cannot change, it is only too apparent that it can be forgotten.

The downward cascading of the last phase of the Kali-Yuga (the "end times") reveals itself — and in riotous pro-fusion — in the "falls" mentioned above: the Renaissance, the Enlightenment, the French Revolution, the Industrial Revolution, the machine age (leading ultimately to the technological age), the advent of the legion of 19th-, 20th-, and 21st-century "antichrists" (who, either simultaneously or in quick succession, unleashed an unprecedented undermining

---

[5] These two items have been placed within quotation marks, for the science and reason envisaged by the secular humanists have little to do with the *scientia* and *ratio* of Greco-Roman and Medieval philosophy.

of faith), the hippie "revolution" and, to cap it all, the Vatican II Council.[6]

This "last phase" of the Kali-Yuga is within living memory: the two world wars, communism, nazism, Hiroshima and Nagasaki. But it is also with us every day: in even more recent times, "terrorism" and "ethnic cleansing" have cropped up all over the place; and finally, following upon the attack on New York in September 2001 — and the fundamentally misplaced reaction thereto — there is the world-wide upsurge of what is daubed "Islamic terrorism". Yes, a "Dark Age" indeed; it is a story of unremitting darkness, in terms of both impiety and suffering. A vain, but stubborn, belief in "progress" can do nothing to alter this.

It is incontestably a downward spiral — and apparently without end. What consolation, what hope, can there possibly be?

Whether we understand them or not, we can, in this context, bring to mind the words of Frithjof Schuon: *La miséricorde perce partout* ("Mercy breaks through everywhere"). Can this possibly be true? Well, let each one of us implacably and objectively consider what these words may mean.

The following examples of mutual recognition and respect between two important religions powerfully manifest that "Mercy that breaks through everywhere". May they help us to understand — and to resist and inwardly elude — the menacing "signs of the times".

This compilation is a message of hope and of trust in God.

William Stoddart

---

[6] My severe comments on the Vatican II Council are presented here without the necessary background explanation. For a full treatment of this question, see *The Destruction of the Christian Tradition* by Dr. R. P. Coomaraswamy (World Wisdom Books, Bloomington, Indiana, 2006) and, for a summary, see *Invincible Wisdom* by myself (Sophia Perennis, San Rafael, CA, 2008), pp. 97-105.

CHRISTIAN ATTITUDES TOWARDS ISLAM

The Gospels and the Acts of the Apostles

The Gospels and the Acts of the Apostles
Fundamental Principles and Guidelines

Other sheep I have that are not of this fold.

John, 10, 16

In my Father's house are many mansions.
(*This applies not only in Heaven, but also on earth*: Sicut in Caelo **et in terra**.)

John, 14, 2

[*After speaking with the Roman Centurion*] Verily I say unto you, I have not found such great faith, no, not in Israel. And I say unto you that many shall come from the east and the west, and shall sit down with Abraham and Isaac and Jacob in the kingdom of Heaven. But the children of the kingdom shall be cast out into outer darkness: there shall be wailing and gnashing of teeth.

Matthew, 8, 10-11

A man's foes shall be they of his own household.

Matthew, 10, 36

When ye see a cloud rise out of the west, ye say, There cometh a shower; and so it is. And when ye see the south wind blow, ye say, There will be heat; and it cometh to pass. Ye hypocrites, ye can discern the face of the sky and of the earth, but how is it that ye do not discern this time?

Luke, 12, 54-56

And Peter opened his mouth and said: 'Truly I perceive that God shows no partiality, and that anyone in any nation who fears Him, and does what is right, is acceptable to Him'.

Acts of the Apostles, 10, 34-35

The Virgin Mary

The House at Ephesus (*Meryem Ana Evi*)

This House, near Ephesus in Turkey, is believed by many Christians and Muslims to be the place where the Virgin Mary lived following the Crucifixion; she fled there from Jerusalem with St. John the Evangelist to escape the wrath of the Jews. Many believe that Ephesus is the place of the Assumption or Dormition; some, however, believe that this took place in Jerusalem to which, it is said, Mary returned shortly before she died. During the many years that she lived in Ephesus, she was visited by several of the Apostles, apart from St. John who is said to have accompanied her to Ephesus.

In Turkish, the House is called *Meryem Ana Evi* ("the House of Mother Mary") or *Panaya Kapulu* ("the Chapel of the All-Holy"). The discovery of the house, and its authentification, have been described by the German poet Clemens von Bretano (1778-1842) and later, and more fully, by two Lazarist missionaries from Smyrna (Izmir).

In modern times, this house is visited by bus-loads of Turkish Muslims — including bus-loads of children — on Turkish public holidays. Many of them walk quietly around the house praying silently. Some say the formal Muslim prayers, depending on the time of day.

The house is owned and administered by the Roman Catholic Church, and a priest and some nuns live nearby. The house, in fact, has been arranged as a small chapel with an altar, and mass is said there every day. There is a room in the house (the one that was Mary's bedchamber) in which Muslims can say the formal Muslim prayer. The prayer mats are provided by the church. The priest frequently has occasion to meet the Turkish individuals and groups who visit, and talks to them about the history of the House,

Many Catholics from Western Europe, and also Orthodox from Greece, Russia, and other Eastern European countries, make pious visits to this house; likewise do many Protestants.

A spring emerges from under the house which is believed to have healing properties. Many votive offerings and tokens have been left at the House by Muslims, Catholics, and Orthodox, who, after drinking the water, or making prayers to the Virgin, have received favors or cures.

The basilica built in honor of St. John and containing his tomb is nearby, as is also the large, ancient mosque called the Mosque of the Lord Jesus.

Ephesus is a center of pilgrimage for both Christianity and Islam. At Ephesus, the Virgin brings blessings to Christians and Muslims without distinction.

An outward sign of the spirit of Ephesus is the good attitude of the priest and nuns towards Muslims, and the good attitude of both the Turkish authorities and the Turkish people, firstly towards the shrine of the Virgin Mary as such, and secondly towards the Christian presence and the Christian pilgrims. (*See Illustrations (2) and (3) on pp. 103-104.*)

Roman Catholic

Popes

Pope Pius XI (1857-1939)

The following words were uttered by Pope Pius XI when dispatching his Apostolic Delegate to Libya in 1934:

Do not think you are going among infidels. Muslims attain to salvation. The ways of Providence are infinite.

L'Ultima (Florence), Anno VIII, 1934

*
* *

Pope Pius XII (1876-1959)

In the 1950s, Pope Pius XII declared:

How consoling it is for me to know that, all over the world, millions of people, five times a day, bow down before God.

Roman Catholic

Cardinals

Nicholas of Cusa, Cardinal of St. Pierre-aux-Liens (1401-1464)

To different countries Thou hast sent different prophets and different masters, the ones at one time, the others at another time. But it is a law of our condition as men of this earth that a long habit becomes for us second nature, that it is taken for a truth and defended as such. It is from this that great dissensions arise, when each community opposes its own faith to other faiths.

And if it should be that it is impossible to remove this difference as to rites, and that this difference should even seem desirable in order to increase devotion (each religion attaching itself with more devotion to its ceremonies as if they had the more to please Thy Majesty), nevertheless, at least, as Thou art unique, there is but one religion and one worship.

From *De Pace Fidei*, 6 (1450)

Cardinal Tisserant, Dean of the Sacred College of Rites (1884-1972)

At the present time, when materialistic neo-paganism is striving to compromise and destroy spiritual values, may the example of the faith of Abraham give courage to all those who have learned to admire it — Jews, Christians, and Muslims — by inspiring them with an invincible trust in the Omnipotence of Him Who wishes only to answer the prayers of those who pray to Him.

From the Preface to the June 1951 number of *Cahiers Sioniens*, which was devoted to *Abraham, Father of Believers*

Roman Catholic

Bishops

The Roman Catholic Bishops of Nigeria

The closing words of the first Joint Pastoral Letter of the Nigerian Roman Catholic Bishops since Nigerian independence:

We express sentiments of fraternal love towards our Muslim fellow-citizens.... We appreciate their deep spirit of prayer and their striking fidelity to penitential fasting.... We are united against tendencies towards materialism and secularism.

Catholic Herald (London), 21st October 1960

The Bishop of Gerona (died 954) and Prince Al-Hakam (died 976)*

One of the prejudices most calculated to hinder an understanding of the development of culture in the Catalan region is to believe that between Christians and Muslims there were no contacts other than those of the battlefield. A state of war was neither permanent nor general ... and it was never a case of annihilating the enemy, but merely of wresting from him the most important booty.

Commercial relations between Christians and Muslims were constant; travelers in the two regions crossed the frontier; the ambassadors of our princes would often arrive at the court of Córdoba which was as resplendent as that of the Emperor of Byzantium; the armies, commanded by princes and bishops, entered the service of the Muslims, even to fight against other Christians.

Nothing could be more false than to imagine a permanent crusade, when very often there were peaceful and even friendly relations. This term is not too strong when we know that Gotmar II, who was bishop of Gerona from 940 to 954, dedicated one of his works to Prince Al-Hakam, son of the Caliph 'Abd ar-Rahmân III. This was the *Chronica gesta Francorum* or, more exactly, a genealogical series from Clovis to Louis IV d'Outremer (481-939), in which the author goes out of his way to indicate events having a close connection with Muslim history. Written in 940, it was found eight years later at Fostat in Egypt by the Arab historian Al-Massadé, who abridged it in chapter 35 of his *Golden Meadows*. It is certain that the friendship of Bishop Gotmar and the family of the Omayyads dated from a journey made by the prelate to the city of Córdoba. When, and in what role? Perhaps as ambassador, but we have

---

* From Nicolau d'Oliver, *La Catalogne à l'époque romane* [*Catalonia in the Romanesque period*] (Leroux, Paris, 1932), p. 185.

no details. At any rate, the marvelous casket, covered in embossed silver and ornamented with enamel, which is conserved in the Cathedral of Gerona and bears the name of Al-Hakam, is perhaps a testimony of the gratitude of the prince for the bishop's historical work.

The Bishop of Tripoli[*]

Jemberié (my servant) was much astonished when, opening the door one evening, he found himself face to face with the Bishop of Tripoli, who had come to visit me. The idea that such a high dignitary was ready to enter a newly whitewashed *fonduq* quite upset him, since he could not decide which was the greater: the honor of such a visit or the shame of being obliged to receive such an eminent person in a hut until recently used only by camel-herds. The Apostolic Vicar, however, was not bothered by such considerations.

He was a man of over fifty, thickset, obese, and short-necked. He looked at people through half-closed eyes behind thick glasses, his nose raised like a hound on the scent and his fingers, on one of which he wore the episcopal ring, combing his bushy beard. After he had listened to an argument and made up his mind about it, he would join his hands as if in prayer and in a deep ponderous voice would define the situation or give his view in a few precise and unadorned phrases which admitted no further argument.

He had an excellent knowledge of Hebrew, Arabic, Persian, Turkish, and Albanian. No one in the whole city, with the exception of the head of the Muntasser family, was able to converse with him in classical Arabic, which was a delight to hear. When the chief's nephews were present, they listened open-mouthed without understanding a word, and the Bishop would turn to the chief and, speaking in the local dialect, say that he was astounded to find young Muslims unable to understand their own tongue; feigning indignation, he would call attention to the fact that he, a Christian and foreigner, knew Arabic better that they, who were Arabs and Muslims. The old

[*] From *A Cure of Serpents* by the Italian Duke Alberto Denti di Pirajno, Governor of Tripoli in 1941, and a medical doctor (Pan Books, London, 1957), pp. 151-160.

Muntasser was greatly diverted and rubbed his hands with glee at their discomfiture.

Islamic canonical law held no mysteries for the Bishop; his knowledge of it was such that the High Court often submitted to him the most complicated questions and asked for his opinion.

The first time he invited me to his house he refused to let me examine him, talked to me of his diabetes as though it had no connection with him, and finished by telling me the history of Muhyi 'd-Dîn Ibn 'Arabî, a famous Arab mystic of about the year 1200, of whom I had never heard, but of whose life he knew every detail.

I had already lost the thread of this story when the *Kâdî* entered with a packet of papers under his arm. They put their heads together and began to talk rapidly in lowered voices. The papers were passed from one to the other, turned over and back, while with their forefingers they ran along the lines of the text, stressing phrases and words. Every now and again the Bishop struck the papers with the back of his hand, exclaiming that there was no doubt at all: the case was exactly that. The *Kâdî* assented and then whispered some suggestion which started the examination of the case all over again.

*

*   *

For some reason or other the Bishop took a liking to me. The incorrigible vulgarity of my speech in Arabic amused him. In a fruity voice, with his hands on his hips, he would ask me in what low haunts I had picked up such unorthodox expressions.

He had an exceptional capacity for seeing the grotesque and humorous situations, and this contrasted strangely with his grave appearance, his dignified bearing, and his solemn episcopal vestments with their amethyst-colored buttons.

The Jewish community had as its head a Rabbi who was universally respected for his integrity and the soundness of his doctrine. This worthy Talmudist was afflicted with a nose of such melancholy proportions that it overhung his mouth. He had such a permanently desolate expression that he always seemed to have just left the Wailing Wall. I asked the Bishop why the Rabbi had such an unhappy air and what could be done to console him.

"Nothing," he replied, with a grave shake of his head, "absolutely nothing. This man, who knows the Talmud as very few know it, has every reason to look like that. I wonder how many times you have pulled a long face waiting for a train that was half an hour late. Well, you can hardly expect light-heartedness and jollity from someone who has been waiting thousands of years for the Messiah."

*

* *

It was the same Bishop who introduced me to his best friend in the town — the Arab mayor of Tripoli.

The friendship between the Bishop and the pasha was one of the most extraordinary I have ever seen. I have never met two men who were, on the surface, more directly opposed in temperament, and rarely have I come across a deeper and closer friendship. The Italian was of modest origin, the Arab the head of a princely family which had once ruled the country; the Bishop held to the simple and pure faith of St. Francis of Assisi, the prince was a fervent and practicing Muslim; the humble Christian had an encyclopedic erudition, the Muslim nobleman was unlettered.

The pasha never refused alms to a beggar, but if the beggar addressed him as *Sîdî* ("my Lord"), he would say: "Your Lord, my Lord, is Allah." He was not rich, but every day food for about forty poor people was prepared in his kitchen.

I had often asked the Bishop about his friendship with the pasha, endeavoring in my curiosity to discover on what it was based. He was always evasive in his reply; sometimes he did not reply at all, and confined himself to raising his shoulders and blowing into his beard.

The more I came to know the Arab nobleman, however, the more I discovered what they had in common — for example, their indifference to illness, their complete disregard of material considerations, their deep understanding of human suffering and misery, and their charity, which was unbesmirched by egoism and knew no limits. Both of them submitted to a higher Will with the blind faith of children.

At a certain point I realized that, just as the various elements in a mosaic form a single design when pieced together, so the mental attitudes of the two friends were part of a single spiritual conception which I was at last able to recognize.

One day, as I was helping the Bishop to put his books on his library shelves, I announced that I had finally understood why he and the pasha were such close friends; I said that their friendship was a friendship between Franciscans. He continued to turn the pages of a volume he held in his hand, as though seeking a reply there. After a few moments of silence he closed the book, and said: "You express yourself badly. You ought to know that a Muslim cannot be a Franciscan friar, and I myself am too unworthy of the robe I wear to call myself a Franciscan. The pasha is a man of great heart and exemplary humility who practices the three canonical virtues in a most admirable manner.... I have learned much from this man; that is why we are friends."

The younger of the two friends died first. I was far away from Tripoli when it happened, and only later did I learn how the Apostolic Vicar had died serenely, surrounded by his *confrères* and nuns, gripping the hand of his old friend the pasha, who in sorrow turned to stone; while in the cathedral, the mosque, and the synagogue, men of different faiths prayed that God would postpone the appointed hour.

> *It seems highly probable that it was to this Bishop of Tripoli that Pope Pius XI, in 1934, addressed the words quoted on p. 12.*

Roman Catholic

Monks

Adelhard of Bath

(12th century English Benedictine Monk)

Lest it be thought that one as ignorant as I have fashioned these thoughts for myself, I do declare that they derive from my studies of the Arabs. I do not wish — should anything I say displease certain limited minds — to be the one who displeases them, for I know full well what the truly wise must expect from the common run of men. Therefore I take care not to speak for myself; I speak only for the Arabs.

The Monk and the Caliph
The Story of a 10th century German Benedictine Monk and
'Abd ar-Rahmân III (reigned 912-961)*

'Abd ar-Rahmân's patient and subtle handling of a particularly obstinate ambassador provides a case-history that might profitably be studied by any budding diplomat set on attaining a higher than average competence in his profession. The date is 957, when an embassy was sent to 'Abd ar-Rahmân III by Otto the Great, King of Germany and later Emperor. The central point that arose was really the same as that of the old puzzle: "What happens when an irresistible force meets an immovable object?" Clearly there is no answer; the only hope is to stop them from meeting, and that is what caused the Caliph so much trouble, for although in its own sphere his power was irresistible, the will of the monk in the story was no less immovable.

The deadlock came about thus. For reasons which are not known, 'Abd ar-Rahmân had sent an embassy some years before to the "great chief of Alemanya". The letter he sent contained the usual phrases about the greatness of the Western Caliphate, but they went too far, and contained some expressions displeasing to Christian ears. As 'Abd ar-Rahmân was neither a fool nor a fanatic, it is likely that the objectionable passages were due to the blunder of a Court official, but they enraged King Otto, who detained the ambassadors for three years, while steadily refusing to enter into further relations with them.

However, something had to be done, and so Otto determined to send a counter-embassy, not so much to deal with political affairs as to retort in kind to the passages in which the Caliph's letter gave offense. The letter was composed by

---

* Extracted from *Spain under the Crescent Moon* by Angus Macnab (Fons Vitae, Louisville, Kentucky, 1999), pp. 62-70.

Otto's brother, St. Bruno the Great, Archbishop of Cologne, in the same language as that of the Caliph's letter, namely Greek, regarded as the intermediary language between Arabic and Latin, and it returned insult for insult; accordingly a stout-hearted messenger was required, a man not afraid to face the Caliph's wrath.

A monk named John from the Benedictine Abbey of Gorze (or Görtz) in Alsace-Lorraine volunteered for the mission, fully prepared to sacrifice his life if need be (*Johannes sese offert spe martyrii*); he later became abbot of the monastery and is canonized as St. John of Gorze. With him, as companion, went a disciple named Garamannus (?Hermann), who wrote an account of the whole mission. In spite of the disobliging letter, Gorze Abbey itself provided rich gifts for the monk to take to the Caliph.

The two monks traveled on foot as far as Vienne, where they took shipping down the Rhône and thence across by sea to Barcelona. The first Muslim city they came to was Tortosa, where the governor treated them with great consideration and assisted them to make the rest of their journey to Córdoba.

On arrival there, they were lodged in a house two miles from the royal palace, and treated with regal generosity, but were not invited to present their letters of credence. Their state was in fact one of luxurious imprisonment. When they asked the reason for the delay, they were told that since the Córdoban ambassadors had been detained for three years in Germany, they would be detained for nine years in Córdoba. In fact, however, the Caliph was stalling for time in order to decide what to do. He had really got himself into an impossible position, for he had a very fair idea of what was in the letters, and so, unfortunately, had some of his subjects. Now, if he received the ambassadors and let them read their letters, he would be bound to charge them with offenses against Islam and the Prophet. Yet to kill a guest, even if he be your worst enemy — not to speak of an ambassador — is a crime in Muslim eyes. On the other hand, if he listened to the letters without retaliation, he would be committing a crime himself, for the law said that anyone who tolerated blasphemy was just as guilty as the actual blasphemer. If this applied to all Muslims, however humble, what of the Caliph himself, the Commander of the Faithful? Further undesirable consequences might include tension with the Christians and, at the worst, a war with the German empire!

After much thought, the Caliph commissioned a leading Jew, as a neutral third party, to try and persuade the monks to visit the Palace but without presenting their documents. John refused, and the two monks were left in solitude for some months more. The next visitor they had was the Mozarabic bishop of the Christians in Córdoba. As the Mozarabic bishop and the German monk could talk freely in Latin, we possess an account of the conversation, which throws an interesting light on the state of the Church under Muslim overlordship at that time. The two clerics first spoke of all manner of things, but finally the bishop revealed the real reason for his visit, namely 'Abd ar-Rahmân's desire to receive the embassy with its presents only.

"And what shall I do with the letters?" asked John. "Have I not been sent especially to deliver them? He was the first to utter blasphemies, and all we do is to refute them."

The text is not complete, but we can read a great part of the bishop's reply:

"You do not know the conditions under which we live. The Apostle forbids us to resist the powers of the world.... It is a great consolation to us ... to live according to our own laws.... The most fervent observers of the Christian precepts are regarded most highly, whereas the Jews [who did not recognize the Messiah] are disparaged by both communities. Our situation demands from us the conduct we follow, and we do nothing contrary to our religion. In other respects we behave obediently, and that is why I think it would be better to suppress that letter, which may needlessly arouse passions against you and us."

John hesitated for a moment, but speedily rallied, and refused to give way:

"How can you use such language, you who purport to be a bishop? Are you not a confessor of the faith, and have you

not been raised to the post you hold in order to defend it?...
Yet for human considerations you depart from the truth, and
far from urging the rest to proclaim it, you yourself evade your
duty. Better would it have been, and more proper for a truly
Christian man, to suffer all the straits of misery, rather than to
accept from the enemy a nourishment prejudicial to the salvation of others."

John then criticized a number of the practices of the
Mozarabic church. "How can you possibly live such a life? I have
heard that you submit to what the Catholic Church regards as
odious: I have been told that your people circumcise themselves despite the command of the Apostle, and abstain from
certain foods, merely because their doctors forbid them."

"Necessity constrains us," replied the Bishop, "otherwise
we could not live among our conquerors, and besides, all that
we do was already done by our forefathers, and their usage has
taught us to do the same."

"Never," said John, "can I approve the doing of anything
other than what is commanded, whether from love or from
fear." And he added that nothing in the world would make him
waver in his resolution. When this was reported to the Caliph,
who was a man well skilled in working on the human heart, he
let some time pass before trying to do anything else.

Six or seven weeks later, when further messengers from the
Caliph had met with no better success, and it was clear that
personal threats would be of no avail, it was hinted to John that
his attitude might bring down a general persecution on the
Christians. Garamannus relates the affair as follows:

"On the Lord's day and on certain of the principal feasts
of our religion, such as Christmas, Epiphany, Easter, the
Ascension, Whitsun, St. John's and some others, the Christians
were allowed to repair to a church outside the city dedicated
to St. Martin," and undoubtedly they must have done so in procession, for he states that they were afterwards accompanied by
twelve guards, whom he calls *sagiones*, from the church back to
the city. John had obtained leave to go with them, and on the
way a messenger handed him a letter — remarkable for its size,
for it was written on a square sheepskin — making the threats

mentioned above. However, not even this made the monk deviate from his purpose.

Finally, the Mozarabic Christians themselves approached him to try to find a solution. John then suggested the only possible one, namely to send a messenger to King Otto with full information, and to ask for further instructions. The Caliph agreed, but as he could not find anyone ready to undertake such a long and hazardous journey, he published an edict offering a special boon to anyone who would volunteer to go, and all manner of rewards on his return.

In the palace secretariat was a Christian official called Recemundus (Raimundo), who was renowned for his perfect knowledge of Arabic and Latin. He was duly attracted by the possibility of preferment, but before volunteering, he applied for leave to visit the ambassador in order to find out what manner of man Otto was, and whether, if he went, he was likely to be imprisoned himself in revenge for the detention of Otto's ambassador in Córdoba. John assured him that he need have no apprehension on these points, and gave him letters of recommendation to Gorze Abbey. Raimundo returned to the palace prepared to undertake the embassy, but requested that he be presented to the bishopric of Iliberis, which was then vacant. The Mozarabic authorities agreed and Raimundo was consecrated bishop. He was provided with the necessary instructions, and set out on his journey. In ten weeks he arrived at Gorze, where he was well received. It was then August, and the Bishop of Metz kept him there during the autumn and winter, and then accompanied him to the Emperor's court at Frankfurt. Otto was probably glad enough to call the whole thing off, and agreed to all that was suggested; a new letter was composed, and Raimundo was back at Gorze by Easter, and at Córdoba by June 959, accompanied by the new ambassador, Dudo. The new letter authorized John not to present the former one, but instead to negotiate a treaty of friendship and peace, to put an end to the incursions of Arab pirates and filibusters who were causing a great deal of trouble in imperial territories, including southern France, Lombardy, and even Switzerland. These were simply bands of adventurers who had got across into Provence from Catalonia, and the Córdoba emirate had never given them any protection or encouragement.

The new ambassadors presented themselves at the palace, but 'Abd ar-Rahmân said: "No, by my life; let the former ambassadors come first; no-one shall see my face before that courageous monk who has defied my will for so long!" But even now, there were still difficulties. When the viziers arrived at the monk's house to conduct him to the palace, they found him with his hair and beard uncombed and in the penitential monastic robe. This would not do, the officials said, and the Caliph sent him a gift of ten pounds of silver to buy a court dress. John returned thanks, but gave the money to the poor. "I do not scorn the gift of kings," he said, "but I cannot wear any other dress than the habit of my order." When the Caliph heard this, he exclaimed: "Let him come however he likes, even if clad in a sack; I shall not receive him the less well for that!"

So at last the interview took place. The monks were led to the palace with immense splendor through streets lined with troops in gala uniform, and preceded along the road by dancing dervishes. "It was the summer solstice," writes Garamannus, "and from the city to the palace these Moors never ceased to raise a fearful dust." He was of course unaware of the true nature of the sacred chant of the dervishes (the Persian word *darvish* being the equivalent of the Arabic word *faqîr*, meaning "poor man", in the same sense as the "holy poverty" of the Franciscans), and of the high honor being rendered thus by the representatives of one religion to those of another.

The chief dignitaries of the Caliphate came out to meet the Christian ambassador, then led him through dazzling saloons into the presence of the Caliph, who now, almost at the end of his reign of half a century, appeared very seldom in public, and "like a god" (*quasi numen quoddam*) hid himself from the eyes of his subjects. Amid surroundings of untold riches, the Caliph sat cross-legged upon a couch; he gave John the palm of his hand to kiss, an honor which Muslim princes reserved only for the greatest of lords. As a Christian, the monk was given an armchair to sit in (Muslims generally sitting on the carpeted floor), and after a prolonged silence 'Abd ar-Rahmân began to speak of the reasons which had obliged him to delay this interview for so long. John replied, and a conversation ensued, in which the Caliph proved so courteous and amiable that he won John's heart despite the natural prejudice with which the monk had approached him. The presents were offered and accepted, and the monk asked leave to return to his own country; but 'Abd ar-Rahmân would not permit him to do so until he had seen John several times more and got to know him better.

In the growing acquaintanceship John developed a deep affection for the Caliph, and he returned from the palace to his sumptuous lodging convinced that the Arabs "did not deserve the name of barbarians that they were constantly given in Europe". At subsequent interviews, now on more familiar terms, they discussed questions of state. The Caliph inquired minutely concerning the power, wealth, and military affairs of Otto; he debated many points with John, who would not allow that anyone was Otto's superior in arms and horses. In this, 'Abd ar-Rahmân praised his staunchness, but criticized Otto's conduct in leaving unpunished the rebellion of his son and son-in-law, who had not hesitated to call in the Hungarians to ravage the empire they sought to usurp.

As to the rest, and the agreements, if any, that were concluded between the two empires, we are not told, for the chronicle of Garamannus ends at this point; but one thing is certain: before St. John of Gorze (the "immovable object") returned home, he had conceived as great a respect and admiration for 'Abd ar-Rahmân (the "irresistible force") as 'Abd ar-Rahmân already had for him.

Roman Catholic

Kings and Knights

Sicily in the Norman Period (approx. 1070-1200)

In 827, the Arabs (also known as Saracens or Moors) entered Sicily from North Africa, and gradually, by 843, took over the whole of the island, wresting control of it from the Byzantine Emperor. The Italian historian Vincenzo Salerno records that under the Arabs religious tolerance prevailed and there were no forced conversions to Islam; he mentions that the minority communities (Christians and Jews) were taxed by the Muslim administration, but opines that many Sicilians probably welcomed the change, as they had been overtaxed by their Byzantine rulers.

Salerno continues: "The Arab influence was nothing short of monumental. Under their administration, the island's population doubled as dozens of towns were founded and cities repopulated, notably Palermo, which became one of the largest and most beautiful of Arab cities after Baghdad and Córdoba. The Arabic language was widely spoken and was a major influence on Sicilian speech, which finally emerged as a Romance (Latin) language during the subsequent (Norman) era. Until the arrival of the Arabs, the most popular language was a dialect of Greek. Under the Arabs, Sicily became a polyglot community; some localities were Greek-speaking, while others were predominantly Arabic-speaking. Mosques stood alongside churches and synagogues." (*See illustration (8) on p. 109 of a polyglot inscription on a Christian tomb.*)

Islamic influence was particularly visible in the arts. Many examples of this remain extant, notably in architecture. (*See illustration (7) on p. 108 of a sculpted plaque of Koranic verses in Arabic on a column of Palermo Cathedral.*)

Salerno writes: "The Normans conquered Messina in 1061, and reached the gates of Palermo a decade later, removing from power the local emir, but respecting Arab customs. The Normans' conquest of Arab Sicily was slower than their conquest of Saxon England, which began in 1066 with the Battle of Hastings. The Normans' Sicilian kingdom was the medieval epitome of multi-cultural tolerance.

"It is interesting to consider that the general functional literacy among Sicilians was higher in 870 under the Arabs than in 1870 under the Italians. In certain social respects, nineteenth-century Sicily still seemed very Arab, especially outside the main cities, well into the early years of the twentieth century."

The Norman king Roger I (1031-1101) introduced Roman Catholicism to the island, but he continued the Muslim policy of the fruitful co-existence of the two faiths — or rather, of the three faiths, for the Latin King also viewed the Greek Orthodox community with favor.

Roger was succeeded by Simon de Hauteville (1093-1105) in 1101. On the latter's death, only four years later, Simon was succeeded by the celebrated Frederick II (1194-1250), who likewise continued the policy of benign co-existence. Indeed, from late in the 11th century to the end of the 12th century was a golden age of Christian-Islamic symbiosis *under Christian rule*.

After about 1200, however, due to papal jealousy and pressure, things gradually changed, in favor of Roman Catholicism and Latin hegemony.

The Templars

Hugo de Payns (c. 1070-1136) was a French nobleman from the region of Champagne. As a knight he participated in the first crusade in 1096. In 1108, he went to Jerusalem for a second time, and decided to take up permanent residence there. He was the founder of the Order of the Temple of Solomon (the Templars), and its first Grand Master. Together with St. Bernard of Clairvaux (1091-1153), he created the Latin Rule, the code of conduct of that Order.

The Knights Templar, as a military-monastic order, had as their original mission the bringing of the Holy Land under Christian control but, during the 12th and 13th centuries, they were instrumental in creating a climate of respect for the learning and spirituality of Muslim culture, both in Spain and the Holy Land. In these two widely separated locations, they discerned the common ground between the deepest layers of Christian and Muslim civilizations.

Angus Macnab writes: "It is not to be supposed that the Order sprang fully armed, Athena-wise, from the head of Hugo de Payns, or was the child of any individual human intelligence. The professed and official function of the Templars, certainly, had arisen out of the crusades; but clearly there had long been a number of special functions which only it could perform. The interactions between the highest Christian spirituality and the highest Islamic spirituality (Sufism) in the High Middle Ages demanded a wholly sovereign Order, above kings and bishops, not subject to ordinary legislation or even to interdicts and excommunications, and able when necessary to stand apart from both civilizations and to act as mediator or arbiter between them. Such was the role of the Templars, and its beneficial effect showed itself more than once in the history of Medieval Spain." Macnab describes two such events in his book *Spain under the Crescent Moon* (pp. 92-93).[*]

---

[*] For further details on this little known subject, see: *L'Islam et le Graal* by Pierre Ponsoye (Éditions Denoël, Paris, 1957).

Eastern Christian

Bahirâ (6th century Syrian monk)[*]

Abu Tâlib, the uncle of Mohammed, sometimes took him with him on his travels. On one occasion when Mohammed was nine or, according to others, twelve, they went with a merchant caravan as far as Syria. At Bustrâ, near one of the halts where the Meccan caravan always stopped, there was a cell which had been lived in by a Christian monk for generation after generation. When one died, another took his place, and inherited all that was in his cell, including some old manuscripts. Amongst these was one which contained the prediction of the coming of a Prophet to the Arabs; and Bahirâ, the monk who now lived in the cell, was well versed in the contents of this book, which interested him all the more because he felt that the coming of the Prophet would be in his lifetime.

He had often seen the Meccan caravan approach and halt not far from his cell, but as this one came in sight his attention was struck by something the like of which he had never seen before: a small low-hanging cloud moved slowly above their heads so that it was always between the sun and one or two of the travelers. With intense interest he watched them draw near. But suddenly his interest changed to amazement, for as soon as they halted the cloud ceased to move, remaining stationary over the tree beneath which they took shelter, while the tree itself lowered its branches over them, so that they were doubly in the shade. Bahirâ knew that such a portent, though unobtrusive, was of high significance. Only some great spiritual presence could explain it, and immediately he thought of the expected Prophet. Could it be that he had at last come, and was amongst these travelers?

The cell had recently been stocked with provisions, and putting together all that he had, he sent word to the caravan: "Men of the Quraish, I have prepared food for you, and I would that ye should come to me, every one of you, young and old,

[*] Extracted from *Muhammad: His Life Based on the Earliest Sources* by Martin Lings (Inner Traditions, Rochester, Vermont, 2005), pp. 29-30.

bondman and freeman." So they came to his cell, but despite what he had said they had left Mohammed to look after their camels and their baggage. As they approached, Bahirâ scanned their faces one by one by one. But he could see nothing which corresponded to the description in his book, nor did there seem to be any man amongst them who was adequate to the greatness of the two miracles. Perhaps they had not all come. "Men of the Quraish," he said, "let none of you stay behind." "There is not one that has been left behind," they answered, "save only a boy, the youngest of us all." "Treat him not so," said Bahirâ, "but call him to come, and let him be present with us at the meal." Abu Tâlib and the others reproached themselves for their thoughtlessness. "We are indeed to blame," said one of them, "that the son of 'Abdallah should have been left be-hind and not brought to share this feast with us," whereupon he went to him and embraced him and brought him to sit with the people.

One glance at the boy's face was enough to explain the miracles to Bahirâ; and looking at him attentively through-out the meal he noticed many features of both face and body which corresponded to what was in his book. So when they had finished eating, the monk went to the youngest guest and asked him about his way of life and about his sleep, and about his affairs in general. Mohammed readily informed him about these things for the man was venerable and the questions were courteous and benevolent; nor did he hesitate to draw off his cloak when the monk asked if he might see his back. Bahirâ had already felt certain, but now he was doubly so, for there, between his shoulders, was the very mark he expected to see, the seal of prophethood even as it was described in his book, in the selfsame place. He turned to Abu Tâlib: "What kinship hath the boy with thee?" he asked. "He is my son", said Abu Tâlib." "He is not thy son", said the monk, "it cannot be that this boy's father is alive." "He is my brother's son," said Abu Tâlib. "Then what of his father?" said the monk." He died," said the other, "when the boy was still in his mother's womb." "That is the truth,"said Bahirâ. "Take him back to his country, and guard him against the Jews, for by God, if they see him and know of him that which I know, they will contrive evil against him. Great things are in store for this brother's son of thine."

Nestorian Patriarch Ishyob III
(reigned 649-660)

These Arabs fight not against our Christian religion; nay, they defend our faith, they revere our priests and saints, and they make gifts to our churches and monasteries.

*
* *

The Greek Patriarch Michael III
(reigned 1169-1177)

"Let the Muslim be my master in outward things, rather than the Latin dominate me in matters of the spirit. For if I am subject to the Muslim, at least he will not force me to share his faith. But if I have to be under the Frankish rule and united with the Roman Church, I may have to separate myself from God." (Quoted by Sir Steven Runciman in *Schism*, p. 122.)

The historian Derek Baker comments: "Byzantine experience with both Latins and Turks in the twelfth century revealed that the patriarch's prognosis was largely correct."

> *Relations between East and West in the Middle Ages,*
> Edinburgh University Press, 1973

See also: Osman Turan: "Les souverains seldjoukides et leurs sujets non-musulmans" (*Studia Islamica*, I, 1953, pp. 65-100)

*

* *

The Copts

"The private secretary of Saladin (1138-1193) and the head of his war office were both Coptic Christians, as were the Egyptians who defeated the Seventh Crusade."

> From *From the Holy Mountain, Travels in the Shadow of Byzantium* by William Dalrymple (Flamingo, London, 2000)

(For a full discussion on Saladin, see pp. 88-90)

The Monks of Mount Athos

The Eastern Orthodox monastic community on the Mount Athos peninsula in the North-East of Greece still conserves the original statutes or charters granted to Mount Athos by the Turkish sultans. These documents are in beautiful Arabic calligraphy, and always begin with the words: "In the Name of God, the Clement, the Merciful." They guaranteed the monks' religious freedom, and also the independence of the monastic government.

The monastic community flourished under Turkish rule but, as soon as the Turks were expelled from Greece, the monks of Mount Athos began to get grief from the modernistic and secularistic Greek government.

Protestant

A Presbyterian's Experience of Islam

The coach of British tourists sped along a Moroccan highway, spraying with dust the ambling camels, plodding donkeys, and passive pedestrians. Inside the coach the chubby Berber guide pointed out the various points of interest. Mohammed's excellent English (he spoke several languages fluently), his twinkling eyes, long striped robe, dagger in a silver sheath, red fez, and air of benevolence made him the most congenial as well as the most picturesque guide of the tour. One could not help liking him.

Cool trees, shady gardens, bright flowers, white walls — an attractive place. "Ladies and gentlemen, that is the casino. Very nice? It is of course for Hebrews and Christians only."

Later at lunch, Mohammed smilingly refused to help himself from the bottle of wine passed to him from an incoherent Englishman. He returned the courtesy, however, by offering his own beverage, a bottle of mineral water, a gesture which was rejected with an amused snort. Mohammed remained unruffled.

He was quite imperturbable. It did not surprise him to see his passengers gape when a man bowed himself in prayer on the pavement — though he ignored the question "Wot's 'e doin' that for?"

Mohammed knew all about Christians. He had been to England. With his own eyes he had seen how the Christians' religion put no restraint on gambling, drinking, and other things which he, a Muslim, would not do. And so these tourists did not surprise him — the women with their loud laughter and immodest clothes, the men with their arrogant ignorance of non-British civilization — these Christians. Their religion had little to commend it to Mohammed. Not that he would tell them so: better to let them see in him what a Muslim could be.

Would any purpose have been served by protesting to Mohammed that not all Christians frequented casinos, drank to excess, or behaved in an ignorant and unseemly manner? The fact is that in many cases both at home and overseas the word "Christian" now means not so much "belonging to Christ" as "belonging to or following the pattern of Western civilization". The dictionary explanation makes interesting reading covering a scale from "a believer in the religion of Christ" down to "a human being". All manner of things are "christened" — hair styles, cocktails, racing cars, road-houses, poodles. The name of Christ has become so integrated into the English language that its origin is lost or forgotten.

Can anything be done to restore the status of the name by which we, as members of Christ's Church, should be known? Can we rescue it from synonymity with any citizen of the "West"?

E.B.S.
Life and Work, The magazine of the Church of Scotland (Edinburgh), July 1964.

Arthur J. Arberry (1905-1969)
Professor of Arabic at Cambridge University, England*

In making the present attempt to improve on the performance of my predecessors, and to produce something which might be accepted as echoing however faintly the sublime rhetoric of the Arabic Koran, I have been at pains to study the intricate and richly varied rhythms which — apart from the message itself — constitute the Koran's undeniable claim to rank amongst the greatest literary masterpieces of mankind. This very characteristic feature — "that inimitable symphony", as Pickthall called it, "the very sounds of which move men to tears and ecstasy" — has been almost totally ignored by previous translators.

All previous versions of the Koran, like the original text itself, having been written as continuous prose, the rhapsodic nature of its composition has been largely lost to ear and sight; by showing the text as here presented, some faint impression may be given of its dramatic and moving beauty. I have called my version an interpretation, conceding the orthodox claim that the Koran is untranslatable.

There is one feature of antique usage which I have deliberately retained: it is absolutely necessary, if confusion is to be avoided, to mark the distinction between the second person singular and the second person plural.

---

* Extracts from the Preface to *The Koran Interpreted* (1955), a translation of the Koran.

This task was undertaken, not lightly, and carried to its conclusion at a time of great personal distress, through which it comforted and sustained the writer in a manner for which he will always be grateful.

I pray that this interpretation, poor echo that it is of its glorious original, may instruct, please, and to some degree inspire those who read it.

*

*   *

Professor Arberry was an authority on Sufism, and he wrote of the Algerian Sheikh Ahmad al-'Alawî (1869-1934) as one "whose erudition and saintliness recall the golden age of the Medieval mystics".* (*See p. 80.*)

**Luzac's Oriental List*, October-December 1961.

Johann Wolfgang von Goethe (1749-1832)

Here are two unequivocal encomiums of Islam from the illustrious poet.

Spanien

Herrlich ist der Orient
übers Mittelmeer gedrungen.
Nur wer Hafis liebt und kennt,

weiss was Calderon gesungen.

Spain

Most gloriously did the Orient
leap across the Mediterranean.
Only he who knows and loves
Hâfiz,[1]
understands what Calderón[2]
has sung.

Allheit

Gottes ist der Orient!
Gottes ist der Okzident!
Nord- und südliches Gelände
ruht im Frieden seiner Hände.
Er, der einzige Gerechte,
will für jedermann das Rechte.
Sei von seinen hundert Namen
Dieser hochgelobet! Amen.

Universality

God's is the Orient!
God's is the Occident!
Northern and southern lands
rest in peace in His hands.
He who alone is the Just,
wills justice for everyone.
Of all His hundred names,
Let this one be highly praised!
Amen.

from the *Westöstlicher Diwan*
("The West-East Divan")

---

[1] Mohammed Shams ad-Dîn (died 1389), better known as Hâfiz, was the greatest lyric poet of Persia.

[2] Pedro Calderón de la Barca (1600-1681), Spanish dramatist, author of *La Vida es Sueño*.

Cabinet Minister

Colonel Juan Beigbeder, Spanish Foreign Minister

Over this small department (the Spanish Foreign Ministry in 1940) presided Colonel Beigbeder, as romantic a personality as I have ever known. His family was of Breton extraction. He himself had, like many other Spanish officers, made his name in Morocco. "We are all Moors", he once said to me, and certainly his dark, thin Quixotic figure was more in keeping with the Riff and the desert than with the small, stuffy room in which he sat in the Ministry of Foreign Affairs. From time to time the winds of Africa would break into the stifling heat of Madrid and, in the middle of a discussion of high politics, he would start an Arabic chant from the illuminated Koran that always lay on his table.

> From *Ambassador on Special Mission*
> by Sir Samuel Hoare [Lord Templewood]
> (Collins, London, 1946), p. 50

Anecdotalists

Sister Mary Campion (Medical Missionary Sister) *

Farewell, Karachi!

Never shall I forget my last two weeks. I suddenly began to find something to write about everywhere! Even the little donkeys seemed "news" as they jingled past our front gate with bells tied merrily to their knees, and how much more the haughty camel — that good ship of the desert — which goes about with its nose in the air "rising above" the rest of the traffic.

It would be a sad thing too for me to leave all the little *burkha*-clad ladies who throng our clinic and point to their children as "Holy Family". Such lovely children they are: large dark eyes, darkened still more by the shadow of mascara from the day they are born. Solemnly they gaze at one, ear-rings, bangles, necklaces, little ladies dressed in the *silwar* or baggy trousers, and draped with a fine muslin or gauze veil with which they cover their head so gracefully.

Then there were our visits to little Sherif, a small boy whose mother and I had become fast friends ever since I nearly sat on her two-day-old child! How was I to know the little one was buried under the quilt when she asked me to take a seat? Politely she gestured me away. Calmly she lifted the cover, and there she was, little Sa'îda, all of three pounds, warm and moist in her snug little nest. She must have thrived on it, because she is now a healthy two-year-old!

We went there first because we were passing by one evening and the husband asked us to see his wife who had "fever". We went again and again, because the family had now become our friends, and the sight of little Sherif running out from among the big water buffaloes, calling "Sister, Sister", and then pulling our hands to take us back to the little hut he called "home"

---

* "Farewell, Karachi!" (*The Medical Missionary*, Osterley, Middlesex, Vol. 15, no. 3, May-June 1961, p. 41).

was always a wonderful welcome. Sherif has bad eyes, and his mother is not well, but the courtesy and innate refinement of that little home is a lesson to be learned from the East.

Another thing I would miss would be the daily calls to prayer which echo so plaintively through the Muslim city, especially the morning one at dawn, when most of the world is asleep, and we are rising to say our morning prayer, *Prime*. This dawn *adhân*, or call to prayer, from the minarets appropriately ends with the words "Prayer is better than sleep". And it is common to turn a corner in the hospital and suddenly trip over an old lady prostrate on the floor announcing "God is Great!". Or to see our *chowkedar* (gatekeeper) standing silently under the palm tree on our front lawn in the evening, hands crossed in prayer, the darkening sky making a perfect picture.

Then too there were the fishermen. Big, burly men these, our friends from the first. Their wives and daughters are lovely women with a freshness and spontaneity which comes from living close to the sea. How they would dance for us, simple folk dances, clapping their hands and swaying to the sound of the waves in the distance, and to the songs of the East from a group of women who beat out the time on an old drum at their feet.

We take our nurses there for a picnic sometimes, which they enjoy immensely. The fisher-folk give us one of their houses, and with all the chairs they can produce, some straw mats for the floor, and a couple of string beds, it is ours for the day.

At evening, when the fishing boat returns, everyone goes to see the catch and exclaim over it. Last time I went they had even caught a baby shark!

The fish is taken to market daily by camel, and while waiting for the boat to come in, the camels are washed in the sea. It is fun to watch them, groaning and objecting at first, and then suddenly seeming to like the water!

When one of the fishermen's family is sick, they pay us for the hospitalization in fish! Every morning, there is in our front lobby either Ahmed or Ali waiting to hear news of the sick one, and to give us the big fish at his feet!

Truly this was a land of warm-hearted people with a great capacity for friendship, and it was with the scent of its flowers in a garland around my neck, that I waved goodbye to this valiant country which had been my home for four years.

Jerusalem, 1934 & 1937[*]

From the point of view from which I am writing this book, the most important sculpting job I had in these years was the carving of ten panels on the New Museum at Jerusalem — a noble building. This involved my staying in the Holy Land for four months in 1934, and I went again in 1937.

I wish I could properly assess the influence of Jerusalem. I was exceedingly fortunate to have the work there. I'm not particular good at traveling, so unless I've got a job to do, I'd rather stay at home. But at Jerusalem I had work, and a good long job. And it involved my working on the scaffold with Arab workmen. I wore Arab clothes, which means dressing more splendidly than European kings and princes, and hob-nobbed with Laurie Cribb who came with me, in Arab cafés and suqs. It was altogether splendid.

For Palestine is the Holy Land. To me it was like living with the Apostles. It was like living in the Bible. It was the antithesis of everything that our England stands for. I am not saying that there is nothing wrong in Palestine. Wherever there are men, there is sin and violence and selfishness and disease. Moreover, there are poor in Palestine, poorer than anything we can conceive in our up-to-date towns. In spite of all that it is the Holy Land, and they live a holy life, whereas England is unholy and people can only live holy lives in secret.

The English in Palestine and the Jews seem to conceive it to be their mission to reform everything and to turn the Arabs into good Europeans.... Except in the old city of Jerusalem where the streets are only footways, motor cars and motor omnibuses are everywhere.... The smart modern Jews are building smart modern towns and introducing smart modern ways, including smart modern prostitution, and smart modern clothes. Are these things good? They are not.

[*] From *Autobiography* by Eric Gill (1882-1940) (Jonathan Cape, London, 1940), pp. 248-255.

But the discussion of such judgements is beyond the scope of this book. I only want to somehow make it clear that since going to Palestine my mind is pervaded by a different order of living — an order previously only guessed at, but now experienced — an order not only human but essentially holy. "Know ye not that ye are the temple of God and that the spirit of God dwelleth in you? But if any man violate the temple of God, him shall God destroy. For the temple of God is holy, *which ye are.*" "Which ye are!" That is the point....

I am not going to write of the beautiful things ... the beauty of the Judean desert, the beauty of Siloam, the beauty of Justinian's church at Bethlehem, not even the beauty of the Haram at Jerusalem, the Muslim holy place, and the most beautiful place I have ever seen.

Palestine was the last of the revelations vouchsafed to me. It confirmed and enfolded all the others. It was a twofold revelation. In the Holy Land I saw a holy land indeed; I also saw, as it were eye to eye, the sweating face of Christ. The half-ruinous church of the Holy Sepulcher at Jerusalem, the half-ruinous church of the Nativity at Bethlehem, these things are symbolical; and we are incapable of renovating them.... By the inscrutable decree of God, the sweat is not thus to be wiped from his face. He suffers less if the Copts and the Greeks and the Romans quarrel among themselves than if, having abandoned the Cross, they hand the whole notion of salvation to the sanitary authority. That is what our civilization is seeking to do. That has not yet happened at Jerusalem. They have not yet rendered unto Caesar the things that are God's.

Far from finding disappointment in Palestine, I found only good; for I found divine beauty. And it was a double good; for I saw not only the beauty, but also the tears and sweat. Illusion fell away. The nonsensical and illusory grandeurs of Rome: Rome, the Holy City decked out in the finery of ballrooms and banks, the soul-ensnaring magnificence of statistical display, the grand appearance of doctrinal and ethical unity. It seemed to me that we would do better to eschew our grandeurs and forget our numbers — and brag less about our unity while, to the heathen and the pagans and the infidels, the most conspicuous thing about Christians is their sectarian disunity (and this we symbolize with diabolical precision by our bloody fights in the Holy Sepulcher itself — fights stopped only by the police, and Muslim police at that) and their only unity is a merely secular one. For while we fight amongst ourselves about doctrine, we are united in the common worship of money and material success. Here I do not exaggerate. That is the awful thing.

What I am struggling to say is that while I never saw or imagined anything more lovely than the Holy Land — whether you think of it as a land or as human habitations, so also I never saw anything less corrupted by human sin and pride. And I understood as never before the virtue of poverty, and how peace on earth can have no other basis.

ISLAMIC ATTITUDES
TOWARDS CHRISTIANITY

Koran

Koranic Verses relevant to Christianity and Christians

You will find that the best friends of believers [i.e. Muslims] are those who say: "We are Christians." This is because there are priests and monks amongst them, and because they are not proud.

Chapter, "The Table Spread": 5, 85

O People of the Book! Ye have no faith until ye observe the Torah and the Gospel, and all that has been revealed unto you by your Lord.

Chapter, "The Table Spread": 5, 68

Verily, those who believe [i.e. Muslims], those who are Jews, Sabeans, and Christians, and whosoever believeth in the Last Day and doeth good: no fear shall come upon them, nor shall they grieve.

Chapter, "The Table Spread": 5, 69

O People of the Book! Come now to a word common to us and you, so that we worship none but God.

Chapter, "The Family of Imran": 3, 64

Verily We have raised in every nation a Messenger, proclaiming: Serve God and shun false gods.

Chapter, "The Bee": 16, 36

O Mankind! We created you from a single (pair) of a male and a female, and made you into nations and tribes that ye may know each other (not that ye may despise each other).

Chapter, "The Private Apartments": 49, 13

To God belong the East and the West; wheresoever ye may turn, there is the Face of God.

Chapter, "The Cow": 2, 115

[Remember her] who guarded her virginity; We breathed into her of Our Spirit, and we made her and her son a sign for all peoples.

Chapter, "The Prophets": 21, 91

(The "Annunciation", when the Archangel Gabriel came to Mary)

And make mention, in the Book, of Mary. We sent unto her Our Spirit and it assumed for her the likeness of a perfect man. She said: "Lo, I take refuge from thee in the Merciful One, if thou art God-fearing." He said: "I am only a messenger of thy Lord, that I may bestow on thee a faultless son." She said: "How can I have a son when no mortal man hath touched me, neither have I been unchaste?" He said: "So it will be. Thy Lord saith: It is easy for Me; and it will be that We will make of him a revelation for mankind, and a mercy from Us. It is a thing ordained."

Chapter, "Maryam": 19, 16-21

Let the people of the Gospel judge by that which God has revealed to them.

Chapter, "The Table Spread": 5, 47

Those who believe in that which was revealed unto thee (Mohammed), and those who are Jews, Christians, and Sabeans — all who believe in God and do righteous deeds — surely their reward is with their Lord. No fear shall come upon them, neither shall they grieve.

Chapter, "The Cow": 2, 62

Argue not with the people of the Book.... Our God and your God is one and the same.

Chapter, "The Spider": 29, 46

(*Words which the Koran ascribes to the Child Jesus*)

Peace on me the day I was born, and the day I die, and the day I shall be raised alive.

Chapter, "Maryam", 19: 33

There is no compulsion in religion.

Chapter, "The Cow": 2, 256

Mohammed

Some Sayings of the Prophet Mohammed relevant to Christianity

Every son of Adam at birth is touched by satan, save only the son of Mary and his mother.

Whosoever cheats a non-Muslim citizen, or usurps his possessions, I shall be his prosecutor on the Day of Judgement.

One day a funeral procession passed by the Prophet Mohammed, and he stood up as a mark of respect. When he was told that the coffin was that of a Jew, he replied: "Was he not a human being?"

If anyone testifies that there is no god but God, who alone has no partner, that Mohammed is His servant and messenger, that Jesus is His servant and Messenger, the son of His handmaid, His Word which he cast into Mary and a Spirit from Him, and that Paradise and hell are real, then God will cause him to enter Paradise no matter what he has done.

Mohammed and the Icon of the Virgin and Child

Mohammed shields the icon of the Virgin and Child

Inside the Kaaba at Mecca, the walls were covered with the images of idols, which Mohammed's companion Othman was painting over. Amongst them there was an icon of the Virgin Mary and the Child Jesus. Placing his hand protectively over the icon, Mohammed told Othman to efface all the other images, with the exception of one of Abraham.

A Letter of Mohammed

In 628 Mohammed sent a letter of support to the monks of St. Catherine's Monastery at Mount Sinai. The letter mentions the rights accorded to the Monastery, particularly freedom of worship, freedom to own and maintain their property, protection of Christians, and their right to protection in war.

The full letter is as follows:

"This is a message from Mohammed ibn Abdullah, as a covenant to those who adopt Christianity, near and far; we are with them. Verily I, the servants, the helpers, and my followers defend them, because Christians are my citizens; and by Allah, I hold out against them anything that displeases them.

"Neither are their judges to be removed from their positions, nor their monks from their monasteries. No one is to destroy a house of their religion, to damage it, or to carry anything from it to the Muslims' houses. Should anyone take any of these, he would spoil God's covenant and disobey His Prophet. Verily, these are my allies, and they have my secure charter against all that they hate. No one is to force them to travel, or to oblige them to fight. The Muslims are to fight for them. If a Christian woman is married to a Muslim, it is not to take place without her approval. She is not to be prevented from visiting her church to pray.

"Their Churches are to be respected. They are neither to be prevented from repairing them nor the sacredness of their covenants. No Muslim is to disobey the covenant unto the end of the world." (*See also p. 101.*)

The original of this letter came into the possession of the Ottoman Sultan Salîm I, and is conserved in the Topkapi Museum in Istanbul.

The Four "Rightly-Guided" Caliphs

The Four "Rightly-Guided" Caliphs
(*khulafâ rashidûn*)

Of any organized attempt to force the acceptance of Islam on the non-Muslim population, or of any systematic persecution to stamp out the Christian religion, we hear nothing. Had the early Caliphs chosen to adopt either course of action, they might have swept away Christianity as easily as Ferdinand and Isabella drove Islam out of Spain.

> Extract from *The Preaching of Islam: A History of the Propagation of the Muslim Faith* by Thomas W. Arnold (a 19th century Protestant missionary), published in 1896

*
* *

The Caliph Omar (581-644)
The second of the four "Rightly-Guided" Caliphs

It is recorded that, in the early days of Islam, the Caliph Omar refused the invitation of the Orthodox Patriarch of Jerusalem to pray in the church of the Holy Sepulcher, out of fear that, if he did so, the Muslims would henceforth wish to turn it into a mosque.

The Caliph Omar saw some Christian lepers as he passed through Jabiya in Syria. He immediately ordered that they be given a large sum of money from the charity fund and that they should receive their daily dole, meaning that they should be fed free of charge.

The Sufis

Sufism is the inward or mystical dimension of
Islam. The great Sufis of earlier centuries such
as Ibn 'Arabî, Rumi, and Al-Ghazali may be
compared to Christian sages and saints such
as St. Augustine, St. Benedict, St. Dominic,
and St. Francis. Sufi orders can be considered
analogous to Christian monastic orders, except
that the Sufis do not live in monasteries but in
the world.

Ibrahim ibn Adham (died 777)

Ibrahim ibn Adham was born in Balkh, Afghanistan, in the first half of the 8th century. He was a wealthy prince, son of one of the kings of Khorassan. One day when out hunting, he heard a voice saying: "It was not for this that thou wast created." He stopped and said: "A warning has come to me from the Lord of the Worlds." He abandoned his horse, gave his luxurious robe and cloak to a shepherd in exchange for his garments. Henceforth he wandered as a pilgrim from land to land. His conversion from luxury to austerity has often been compared with the story of Prince Gautama, the Buddha.

Ibrahim ibn Adham was one of the earliest of the gnostic or sapiential Sufis. He leaned gnosis from a Christian monk called Father Simeon. Here is his own account:

"I learned gnosis (*ma'rifa*) from a monk called Father Simeon. I visited him in his cell, and said to him: 'Father Simeon, how long hast thou been in thy cell here?' He answered: 'For seventy years.' I asked: 'What is thy food?' He countered: 'O Hanifite, what has caused thee to ask this?' Then he answered, saying: 'Every night one chick-pea.' I said: 'What stirs thee in thy heart, so that this pea suffices thee?' He answered: 'They come to me one day every year, and adorn my cell, and process about it, so doing me reverence; and whenever my spirit wearies of worship, I remind it of that hour, and endure the labors of a year for the sake of an hour. Do thou, O Hanifite, endure the labor of an hour, for the glory of eternity.' Gnosis then descended into my heart." (from *Hilyat al-auliyâ* ["The Chronicle of the Saints"] by Abu Nu'aim al-Isfahânî.)

Muhyi 'd-Dîn ibn 'Arabî (1165-1240)

Muhyi'd-Dîn ibn 'Arabî is generally recognized as one of the greatest of the sapiential or theosophic mystics of Islam. He was born in Murcia in south-east Spain in 1165. He was known as *Muhyi'd-Dîn* ("the Vivifier of Religion") and as *ash-Shaikh al-Akbar* ("the Greatest Sheikh"). Apart from making the pilgrimage to Mecca, he traveled widely in the Islamic world. For a while he lived in eastern Turkey, and the Sultan of Konya showered gifts upon him. Later he went to Aleppo in Syria, where the king, a son of Saladin, also received him with great honor. He finally settled in Damascus, where he died in 1240. His tomb there is venerated to this day. Ibn 'Arabî was a prolific writer, and is celebrated above all for his profound writings in the field of philosophy and metaphysics.

The best known lines from his inspired poetry are the following:

"My heart has become capable of every form: it is a pasture for gazelles, a cloister for Christian monks, a temple for idols, the Kaaba of the pilgrim, the tablets of the Torah, and the Book of the Koran. I practice the religion of Love. In whatsoever directions its caravans advance, the religion of Love shall be my religion and my faith."
Tarjumân al-Ashwâq ("The Interpreter of Love"), XI, 13-15

In his writings Ibn 'Arabî refers to Mohammed as the "Seal of Prophecy" and to Christ as the "Seal of Sanctity. He comments on this as follows:

"The seal of holiness, above which there is no other holy, is our Lord Jesus. We have met several contemplatives of the heart of Jesus.... I have been united to him several times in my ecstasies, and by his ministry I returned to God at my conversion.... He has given me the name of friend and has prescribed austerity and nakedness of spirit."
Al-Futûhât al-Makkîya ("The Meccan Revelations"), II, 64-65

Jalâl ad-Dîn Rûmî (1207-1273)

Jalâl ad-Dîn Rûmî was born in Balkh, Persia, but left at an early age with his father Bahâ'ad-Dîn Walad, a scholar who had had a disagreement with the rulers. After several years of wandering, the family was invited by the Seljuq Sultan of Rûm to settle in Iconium, now Konya, Turkey. To show his respect for Bahâ' ad-Dîn, the Sultan advanced out of the town to meet the scholar as he approached Konya, dismounted from his horse, and led Bahâ' ad-Dîn's mount by the hand into the city. Because of the Byzantine past of the region, it retained the name Rûm ("Rome") among the Turks; and it is from this that Jalâl ad-Dîn came to be known as Rûmî, "the man of Rome [i.e., of the Eastern Roman Empire or Byzantium]".

Rûmî was the author of the *Mathnâwî* ("Rhyming Couplets of Deep Spiritual Meaning"), a vast six-volume work of Sufi teaching, and the greatest treasure of the Persian language. It is the outward expression of the author's inward realization, and also of that spiritual force which lives on to this day in the dervish order which he founded, and which has its center at Konya. Rûmî's disciples referred to him as *Maula-nâ* ("our Master") and the order he founded is called Mevlevi (in Arabic *Maulâwî*). Besides his dervishes (*"fuqarâ"* in Arabic), Rumi also had many Christian disciples.

The members of the Mevlevi order are known as the "Whirling Dervishes" for their dancing and music (*samâ*), both of which are supports for their method of spiritual realization. Apart from the dancing and music of the Mevlevi order, Rûmî is associated with music in other ways, for the singing of the *Mathnâwî* has become an art form in itself

Jalâl ad-Dîn Rûmî famously declared:

"I am neither Christian nor Jew nor Parsi nor Muslim. I am neither of the East nor of the West, neither of the land nor of the sea.... I have put aside duality and have seen that the two worlds are one. I seek the One, I know the One, I see the One, I invoke the One. He is the First, He is the Last, He is the Outward, He is the Inward."

Al-Ghazâlî (1058-1111)

Called by some "the greatest Muslim after Mohammed", Ghazâlî combined theological orthodoxy with mysticism, and scholarship with a profound understanding of the human soul.

Known to Western Europe in the Middle Ages as Algazel, Abu Hamîd at-Tusi al-Ghazâlî, mystic, theologian, and jurist, was born in 1058 at Tus near Meshed in the north-east of Iran. His mother tongue was Persian, but at a very early age, he was taught to master Arabic. He traveled and taught in several places, but died in his birth-place of Tus in 1111.

Al-Ghazâlî was one of those Muslims who knew that the Christian Gospels were entirely valid. He was aware that they had not been "altered", at least in the literal sense understood by many Islamists.

Also, in spite of the general Islamic suspicion of "incarnationism", he had an understanding in depth of the Christian doctrine of the Trinity. This is discussed in detail by Louis Massignon in his article "Le Christ dans les Évangiles selon Al-Ghazali" in *La Revue des Études Islamiques*, 1932, section IV.

The Emir Abd al-Qadir (1808-1883)

"When we think how few men of real religion there are, how small the number of defenders and champions of the truth — when one sees ignorant persons imagining that the principles of Islam are hardness, severity, extravagance and barbarity — it is time to repeat these words: 'Patience is beautiful, and God is the source of all succor'" (*Sabr jamîl, wa 'Llâhu'l-musta'ân*) (Koran, Chapter "Joseph": 12, 18).

Abd al-Qadir, warrior and Sufi, was born in Algeria and died in Damascus. His tomb lay alongside that of Muhyi-d'Dîn ibn 'Arabî in Damascus until his remains were returned to his native Algeria in 1966.

Mulay 'Alî ad-Darqâwî
(a Moroccan Sheikh who flourished
in the first half of the 20th century)

"The text which Mulay 'Alî read aloud to me, and on which he occasionally made brief comments in Moroccan dialect, was a collection of prophecies, partly symbolic and partly literal, which Mohammed and certain of his immediate successors had made with regard to the forthcoming end of the world. Mulay 'Alî had undoubtedly chosen this text in order to show me what Christ meant for him. Indeed, he spoke of Christ's Second Coming as if it were imminent, and at one moment he pointed to himself and said: 'If our Lord 'Isâ (Jesus) should return to earth before I die, I would immediately rise and follow him!'"

From: Titus Burckhardt, *Fez, City of Islam*
(Islamic Texts Society, Cambridge, England;
Fons Vitae, Louisville, Kentucky, 1992), p. 109

Ahmad al-'Alawî (1869-1934) [Algerian Sheikh]

The Sheikh Ahmad al-'Alawî was the 20th century spiritual descendant of the Sheikh Abu'l-Hasan ash-Shâdhilî (1196 -1258), who founded what became known as the Shâdhilî (and later the Shâdhilî-Darqâwî) spiritual order or *tarîqa*. We have already quoted Professor A. J. Arberry, who referred to the Sheikh al-'Alawî as one "whose erudition and saintliness recall the golden age of the Medieval mystics".* The life and teachings of the Sheikh al-'Alawî are to be found in impressive detail in Martin Lings' book *A Sufi Saint of the Twentieth Century.*

A French orientalist wrote of him as follows:

"The Sheikh was always hungry for knowledge about other religions. He seemed to be quite well informed as regards the Christian Scriptures and even as regards the Patristic tradition. The Gospel of St. John and the Epistles of St. Paul appealed to him in particular. As an extremely subtle and penetrating metaphysician, he was able to reconcile plurality with unity in the Trinitarian conception of three Persons in a consubstantial identity."

> From: Augustin Berque, *Un Mystique moderniste*, Revue Africaine, 1936, p. 739, quoted by: Martin Lings, *A Sufi Saint of the Twentieth Century* (London, 1971), p. 82

One of the famous sayings attributed to the Sheikh Al-'Alawî is the following:

> "Truth melteth like snow in the hands of him whose soul melteth not like snow in the hands of Truth."

---

* *Luzac's Oriental List*, October-December 1961.

Sultans and Saints

Abu Walîd: The Muslim Saint[*]

There is one curious feature of the main chapel in Toledo Cathedral which is often allowed to pass unnoticed, though it must be unique among Christian churches. Amid the effigies of saints, holy bishops, and Christian monarchs — defenders of the faith — there stands a fine polychrome statue of an Islamic doctor of theology.

This cathedral was not begun until 1227, and the statue in question, like all the surrounding statuary, is at least a century later; but the memory of this saintly Mussulman was still held in such affection at Toledo that, two hundred and fifty years after his death, his image was set up in one of the two most prominent positions of honor near the high altar.

His name was Abu Walîd, and when the city capitulated to the Christians in 1085, he was the chief *faqîh* (doctor of Islamic law) of Toledo. The *aljama* (in Arabic *al-masjid al-jami'*, namely the "Friday Mosque" or "Congregational Mosque") was the former Visigothic Cathedral of St. Mary, which had been converted to Islamic use when the city fell to Tarik the Berber in 719, and it had been considerably enriched during the intervening three and a half centuries.

When the Moorish king Yahya capitulated to Alfonso VI, the indispensable condition that he stipulated was that the Muslims who chose to remain in Toledo should continue to enjoy the use of the *aljama*. Alfonso accepted this condition and pledged his royal honor to observe it, which in fact he did. But this caused deep discontent among the Christians. By what right, some of them asked, could the king allow the Muslims to debar them, in the heart of their own capital, from the church

---

[*] The following was one of a series of broadcasts, under the general title of "Spain under the Crescent Moon", made by Angus Macnab in the 1950s on the English-language service of the Spanish Radio, and beamed to North America. The episode concerned is also included in Macnab's book *Spain under the Crescent Moon* (Fons Vitae, Louisville, Kentucky, 1999).

which their forefathers had built to the Blessèd Virgin, and she herself had consecrated by a miraculous apparition? The inscription beside the pillar, quoted from the Psalms, read: "Let us worship in the place where her feet have stood." Who was the king to sign away their right to worship there?

On the first occasion when Alfonso had absented himself from Toledo, the malcontents among the people (led by Queen Constanza), and those among the clergy (led by Archbishop Bernardo), came to a secret agreement as to the day and hour for the *coup*, and on 25th October 1087, they forced their way into the *aljama*, dislodged the Muslims, and restored Christian worship there, with Bernardo himself presiding.

The resentment of the Muslims at this breach of faith was exceeded only by the indignation of the king when news reached him of how his solemn pledge had been violated; and he was the more infuriated because he realized that the Muslims might well suspect him of having been privy to the plot. He marched back to Toledo at top speed to punish the authors of the outrage and to enforce the law. The consequences, even for the queen herself, would have been serious, had Alfonso not been intercepted, at the village of Magán, by the aged Abu Walîd and other Moorish notables, who had come out of their own accord to intercede with him.

They gratefully acknowledged his honorable intentions; but, they insisted, if he were to carry them out and restore the mosque to Islam, it could only lead to bitter hatred of the Muslims by the Christians and permanent bad blood between the two peoples; accordingly, they prayed him to take no action and simply let things be. But the king's sense of honor, and the oath he had sworn, would not allow this, and therefore Abu Walîd and his companions formally released the king from his sworn undertaking, and officially renounced the right of their people to the *aljama*.

This prudent and charitable act, loyally supported by the Muslim population, gave Toledo back its cathedral with honor saved on both sides, and from that day onwards the Moors of Toledo lived in perfect peace and harmony with their Christian brethren; even today the architecture and craftsmanship of the city bear witness to the happy brotherhood of artists of the two traditions.

If Abu Walîd is today in Heaven with St. Ildefonso, as I feel sure he is, then he was canonized by the words of Our Lord Himself, when he said: "Blessèd are the peacemakers, for they shall be called the children of God." The saintly *faqîh* stands in his cathedral niche today, not as a mere mark of courtesy, but in his own right, by the grace of God. (*For a photograph of the statue of Abu Walîd, see illustration (5) on p. 106.*)

Ibn Ahmar and St. Ferdinand
(King Ferdinand III of Spain)

When Ferdinand III died in 1252, the Sultan Ibn Ahmar, of the Nasrid dynasty of Granada,* sent his condolences to his son and successor Alfonso X ("Alfonso el Sabio", reigned 1252-1284), along with a hundred Muslim horsemen who, with lighted candles, kept watch over the body of the saintly monarch. Ferdinand was later canonized, and his son, Alfonso the Wise, was one of the most noteworthy of the Christian sages of the Middle Ages.

> From *Spain under the Crescent Moon,* by Angus Macnab (Fons Vitae, Louisville, Kentucky, 1999), p. 179

---

* It was Ibn Ahmar who uttered the famous words, inscribed repeatedly in beautiful calligraphy on the walls of the Alhambra: "There is no victor but God!" (*lâ ghâliba illâ 'Llâh*). On returning home from a successful campaign, the people of Granada greeted him with cries of "Victor! Victor!", whereupon he replied: "There is no victor but God!" This is a variant of the fundamental Islamic credo: "There is no god but God" (*lâ ilâha illâ 'Llâh*).

The Sultan of Egypt, and Moorish Spain
Visits by St. Francis of Assisi (1182 -1226)

It is well known that, at the beginning of the fifth crusade, St. Francis of Assisi, accompanied by several of his brothers, proceeded well beyond the crusader-held territory at the beginning of the fifth crusade, in order to pay a visit to the Sultan Al-Mâlik al-Kamil in Cairo. St. Francis did not make this trip as part of the crusade, in fact, he was in direct opposition to the mainstream, pro-crusade, theological opinions of the time. His purpose, for himself and his companions, was to meet the Muslim people, and live among them as "lesser brothers". In his book *Francis and Islam,* the Dutch scholar Jan Hoeberichts writes: "St. Francis of Assisi stood in complete and unique opposition to the theological justification of the violent methods of Christendom." Dr. Hoeberichts studied philosophy and theology at Franciscan colleges in the Netherlands and Italy, and is a lecturer in moral theology. He also spent 28 years in Muslim areas in the Indian sub-continent.

Mary O'Shaughnessy, of the Episcopal Diocese of New York, basing herself on Dr. Hoeberichts' work, writes: "St. Francis's intention was to live among the people who were being portrayed as evil and as the 'enemies of Christ'. Francis, however, found the spirit of God to be alive and at work within the Muslim people; he admired their public and repeated acknowledgement of God and their call to prayer, and appreciated the deep reverence which they showed to their holy book, the Koran. While the main trend of Christian preachers of that time was to deliver inflammatory sermons against Islam, Francis forbade his brothers to take part in this activity. First and foremost what Francis wanted from his brothers was that they simply live with and among the Saracens."

The visit to Cairo was not St. Francis's only entrée into the Muslim world. Soon after returning from Egypt to Italy, he made another long and arduous journey, this time to Moorish Spain. There is no record that he met with any notable

Bishops or Abbots either in Christian Spain (on his way south) or among the Christian population of Muslim Spain. Christian reports only say that St. Francis's purpose in making this trip remains mysterious, and they are silent regarding whatever he may have done while he was amongst the Moors. They admit, however, that there is no evidence of his having engaged in any evangelizing activity.

Saladin (1137-1193)

Salâh ad-Dîn Yûsuf ibn Ayyûb, known in the West as Saladin, was born of Kurdish descent in Tikrit in what is now Iraq in 1137. He became renowned as a warrior, and is famous above all for the re-taking of Jerusalem from the crusaders in 1187.

Saladin grew up in Balbek and Damascus in Syria. He was a scholar even in his childhood, enthusiastically studying the Koran, theology, and Arab poetry. These early scholarly pursuits continued throughout his life, even when military struggle had become his destiny.

Saladin began his military career by joining the staff of his uncle Asad ad-Dîn Shirkuh, who was the commander of the Syrian army. Shirkuh, accompanied by the young Saladin, led a campaign in the years 1164-1168, to gain lordship over the Shi'ite Fatimid rulers of Egypt. The warring was finally successful and, in 1169, at the age of 32, Saladin was appointed vizier to Al-Adid, the Caliph who was destined to be the last of the Fatimid dynasty. By this time also, Saladin had become supreme commander of the army. On the death of Al-Adid in 1171, he declared the that Shi'ite caliphate had come to an end, and proclaimed a return to Sunni Islam. By 1174, he was the sole ruler of Egypt, and became the first Caliph of the Sunni Ayyubid dynasty. Besides Egypt, Saladin's empire included Syria, Palestine, most of Arabia, and Yemen.

When the crusaders took Jerusalem in 1099, they murdered *all* of its inhabitants, men, women, and children, including the Jews and the large population of non-Catholic Christians; they boasted that parts of the city were knee-high in blood. When, following the battle of Hattin in 1187, Saladin re-took Jerusalem, he and his troops entered the city of Jerusalem with a civility that contrasted sharply with the bloody actions of the crusaders who had conquered Jerusalem eighty years previously. He spared the lives of the vanquished, granted them time to leave, and gave them a safe passage. It was after all, a holy city, and it was captured by the Muslims in a "holy war". When he captured the crusader leaders Guy de Lusignon and Raynald de Châtillon, he spared the life of Guy de Lusignon, but had Raynald de Châtillon executed because, some time previously, he had attacked and killed a group of unarmed Muslim pilgrims on their way to Mecca. Saladin treated all the Catholics, both soldiers and civilians, very well, and the Eastern Christians, who had always opposed the crusaders, even better!

Thus, despite his opposition to the Christian powers, Saladin achieved a great reputation in Europe for his chivalry. He was much admired, and considered to be a model prince. The French author René Grousset writes: "His generosity and his piety devoid of fanaticism — that flower of liberality which had been the model of our old chroniclers — won him no less popularity amongst the crusaders than amongst the Saracens." (*The Epic of the Crusaders*, Orion Press, 1970). Already in the 14th century there was an epic poem about his exploits, and Dante included him amongst the virtuous pagan souls in Limbo. Sir Walter Scott, in his novel *The Talisman*, also portrayed him in a favorable light.

The historian Ismail Abaza writes: "Saladin is a romantic figure in whom it is difficult to find much fault. In fact, some of his most ardent admirers have been his Christian biographers.... What always attracted Europeans to Saladin was his almost perfect sense of cultured chivalry. It is said that the crusader knights learned a great deal about chivalry from him."

The same author writes further: "In his battles against the European crusaders, Saladin often had the aid of Eastern Christians, who were as much the victims of the western armies as anyone else in the eastern lands. The proud Georgians, for example, preferred Saladin to the pope, and so did the Copts of Egypt."

The following incident is related: "In April 1191, a Christian woman's three-month old baby had been stolen from the Frankish camp and sold in the market. The Franks urged her to approach Saladin himself with her grievance. She did so, and Saladin used his own money to buy back the child. An eyewitness of the scene writes as follows: 'He then gave the child to the mother, who took it with tears streaming down her face, and hugged it to her breast. The people were watching her and weeping and I (Ibn Shaddad) was standing amongst them. She suckled her infant for some time, and then Saladin ordered a horse to be fetched for her, and she returned to the Frankish camp'" (From *The Rare and Excellent History of Saladin*, by Bahâ'u 'd-Dîn ibn Shaddad, translated by Donald S. Richards, 1981).

By the time of his death, Saladin had liberated almost all of Palestine from the armies of England, France, Flanders, and Austria.

Saladin died of a fever in Damascus in 1193. When they opened Saladin's treasury, they found that there was not enough money in it to pay for his funeral. He had given away most of it in charity.

The Caliph of Damascus and St. John of Damascus (676-c. 754)

St. John of Damascus, or St. John Damascene, was born in Damascus, and had a high function at the court of the Caliph. It was there that he wrote and published, with the acquiescence of the Caliph, his famous treatise in defense of images — something that he could not have done if he had lived within the Byzantine empire, since images had been forbidden by the iconoclastic Emperor Leo III. In this connection, Metropolitan Kallistos Ware puts it very nicely when he refers to "the safety of his position outside the Empire"! This is not the only occasion that Christians have felt more secure under the Muslims than under Christian authorities. (*See, for example, pp. 40, 41, 42, and 99.*)

The Emir in Turkey and St. Gregory Palamas (1296-1359)

St. Gregory Palamas was held by the Turks for a year, during which time he had friendly discussions with the son of the Emir. In their mutual friendship, there was never any question of the Christian Saint converting to Islam or of the Muslim Prince converting to Christianity.

The Ruler of Tunisia and St. Louis, King of France (1214-1270)

St. Louis, King of France, when he was in Tunisia had amicable discussions with the ruling circles there, without there being any question of "conversion" in one direction or another.

King Mohammed V of Morocco (1909-1961)

This report does not concern Christians but Jews.

During the war years 1940-1942, the Vichy French authorities were coerced by their nazi occupiers to put pressure on the Jews of Morocco, which was then under French rule.

King Mohammed V of Morocco strongly resisted the proposed oppressive measures which the Vichy French tried to enforce. "The Jews are my subjects," he declared, "and they are under my protection."

When the French tried to introduce the nazi practice of forcing Jews to wear a yellow star, the King declared that he would be the first to wear one.

The King's efforts in defense of the Jews of Morocco were gratefully recognized by Jewish authorities after the end of the war.

Historians

From *Maurische Kunst** [*Moorish Art*] by Ernst Kühnel (born 1882)

We see Muslim and Catholic princes not only allied, when the power of a dangerous co-religionist had to be curbed, but also aiding one another generously to suppress disorders and revolts. The reader will learn, no doubt to his surprise, that in one of the battles for the Caliphate of Córdoba in 1010 Catalan forces saved the situation, and on this occasion three bishops gave their lives for the "Prince of Believers" (*amîr al-mu'minîn*). Al-Mansûr had in his entourage several counts who joined him with their troops, and the presence of Christian guards in the courts of Andalusia was by no means exceptional. When an enemy territory was conquered, the religious convictions of the population were respected as far as possible; let us recall only that Mansûr — who was not usually over-scrupulous — took care, at the assault on Santiago, to protect the church containing the tomb of the Apostle from all profanation and that, in many other cases, Caliphs seized the opportunity to manifest their respect for the sacred things of the enemy. In similar circumstances, the Christians had a similar attitude: for centuries Islam was respected in the re-conquered territories, and it was only in the 16th century that it was systematically persecuted and exterminated, at the instigation of a fanatical clergy which had grown too powerful. During the whole of the Middle Ages, on the other hand, tolerance with regard to the others' conviction and respect for the sentiments of the enemy accompanied the incessant battles between Moors and Christians, greatly diminishing the rigors and miseries of war, and conferring on the combats as chivalrous a character as possible. In spite of the linguistic abyss, respect for the adversary as well as high esteem for his virtues — and, in the poetry of both sides, an understanding of his sentiments — became a common national bond. This poetry bears eloquent witness to the love or friendship which often united Muslims and Christians beyond all obstacles.

* Berlin, 1924.

From *La Civilisation des Arabes** by Gustave Le Bon (1841-1931)

Force had no part in the propagation of the Koran, for the Arabs always left those they conquered to keep their religion.... Far from being imposed by force, the Koran was spread only by persuasion. Persuasion alone could induce peoples who conquered the Arabs at a later date, such as the Turks and the Mongols, to adopt it.

The Arab armies never reached Indonesia, and this is the most heavily populated Muslim country in the world. It was the Arab traders — and especially the Sufis amongst them — who converted Indonesia and the Malay peninsula to Islam.

One thinks also of the Mongols who swept away all that was in their path, but who ended up by adopting the religion of the people they conquered.

In Yugoslavia, it was mainly the heretical Bogomil community which, during the period of Turkish rule, converted to Islam. The Serbs remained Orthodox and the Croats remained Catholic.

The falseness of the allegation that Islam was spread by the sword is decisively shown by the fact that the populations of Greece and Spain (both under Muslim rule for several centuries) remained Christian. The monastic community of Mount Athos in the North-East of Greece flourished during the period that Greece was under Turkish rule but, as soon as the Turks were expelled from Greece, the monks of Mount Athos began to get grief from the nationalistic — and secular — Greek government.

* Paris, 1884.

From *Muslim Spain** by Duncan Townson

In Muslim Spain, those who remained Christian were well treated, as they were throughout the Islamic Empire. Both Jews and Christians were regarded as "People of the Book", that is, as people who had their own holy writings, the Old and the New Testaments of the Bible. In Córdoba, the Christians continued to worship in the Cathedral of St. Vincent, though they were not allowed to disturb the Muslims with hymn-singing or bell-ringing.

Muslims and Christians usually got on very well together, lived much the same life, and dressed alike. Muslims took pleasure in attending Christian celebrations and were frequent visitors at monasteries on saints' days. Even warfare did not divide them. Christians in Muslim Spain were loyal to the emir and fought for their Muslim ruler against the Christian kings of the north. In peacetime Christian kings sent their sons to be taught manners at the court of Córdoba. They married their daughters to Muslim princes and these brides became Muslims too.

Arabic language and literature fascinated Spanish Christians, as did Muslim architecture and science. A Christian of Córdoba named Álvaro wrote in 854: "Innumerable are the Christians who can express themselves in Arabic and compose poetry in that language with greater art than the Arabs themselves."

A popular recreation for rich and poor alike was getting together for picnics and garden parties. People in Córdoba had a passion for them and any occasion would do. Marriages and circumcisions — all Muslim boys were circumcised — called for splendid celebrations. Then there were the Muslim and Christian feast days. At the Christian feast of the Epiphany the whole population joined in the torch-lit processions that went on all night. There were saint's day pilgrimages to Christian monasteries where the monks gave lavish hospitality.... The feast days were great occasions.

* Cambridge University Press, 1973, pp. 18, 25.

From *Fez, City of Islam** by Titus Burckhardt (1908-1984)

In medieval Spain, Muslims, Christians and Jews lived side by side in peace, except when purely political problems might crop up. For Moorish rulers, this situation was a natural one, as toleration of Jews and Christians has its root in Islamic law; however, the Christian kings, to whom this law did not apply, also frequently granted their Muslim and Jewish subjects the same right. This was in no wise the result of religious indifferentism, for in those days, religion took precedence over all else. It seems that it was experience which led to this mutual respect, to the presentiment that behind the unfamiliar appearances of another religious form, the same Divine Truth was to be found, and to a willingness to leave judgement on this matter to God. Moreover, in spite of the three dogmatic systems which distinguished the communities from one another, the spiritual world in which they lived was virtually the same: life and death, Heaven and earth, knowledge and the crafts, had for each of them the same meaning and value. It is significant that the spiritual exchange between the Islamic and Christian worlds broke off suddenly with the rationalism of the Renaissance, and that at the same time the intolerance of the absolute Spanish monarchy began: the Jews were forcibly converted or persecuted, and the Moors expelled.

* Islamic Texts Society, Cambridge, England; Fons Vitae, Louisville, Kentucky, 1992, p. 151.

St. Catherine's Monastery, Mount Sinai

St. Catherine's Monastery, located at the foot of Mount Sinai in Egypt where Moses received the Ten Commandments, was built by the Emperor Justinian between 527 and 565. It encloses the Chapel of the Burning Bush, which was built at the order of St. Helena, the mother of Constantine I, at the site where Moses saw the burning bush. Centuries earlier, Alexander, with his vast army, is said to have passed by Mount Sinai. Sinai is mentioned in both the Bible and the Koran, and the site is sacred to both Christianity and Islam.

The monastery is Greek Orthodox. St. Catherine of Alexandria, after whom it is named, was cruelly martyred, and, according to tradition, her remains were taken by angels to Mount Sinai area. Around the year 800, the monks from the Sinai monastery found her remains. The monastery is much frequented by the surrounding nomadic Bedouin, who perform many services for the monks. There is a little mosque, with a minaret, within the monastery walls.*

It is recorded that the monks of St. Catherine's sent a delegation to Medina in 628, to ask for Mohammed's patronage and protection. The request was granted, and a copy of the letter received, purportedly by Mohammed himself, is exhibited in the Icon Gallery.† It proclaims that the Muslims will protect the monks and, furthermore, that the monks will be exempted from paying taxes. So, when the peninsula came under the rule of the Arab conquerors in 641, the monks and their monastery, from the early Arab period onwards, continued undisturbed. Legend has it that Mohammed visited the Monastery on one of his early journeys as a merchant.

---

* *See illustration (1) on p. 102.*

† *See also p. 70.*

Centuries later, in 1517, the Ottoman Sultan Selim I became, for the monks, a new protector. The Turkish authorities respected the rights of the monastery and even accorded a special status to the Archbishop, who was also the Abbot.

The monastery library contains a vast number of early codices, as well as many manuscripts in Hebrew, Syriac, Greek, Arabic and Coptic. The museum, for its part, houses an immense number of early mosaics and icons. This large collection begins with a few icons dating as far back as the 5th and 6th centuries. These survivals are unique, because the monastery itself is unique in that it completely escaped the ravages of the 8th and 9th century iconoclastic Byzantine emperors. It is a paradox that "iconodulia" has on several occasions been preserved because of the overlordship of "an-iconic" Semitic monotheists.

For centuries, the local Bedouin have frequented the monastery, helping in the garden and cooking. For this they receive from the monks wheat and other sustenance.

St. Catherine's Monastery at Mount Sinai has for long been a center of pilgrimage for both Christians and Muslims.

> Extracted from *The Monastery of St. Catherine* by Dr. Evangelos Papaioannou (published by St. Catherine's Monastery [no date])

ILLUSTRATIONS

"One picture is worth a thousand words"

(1) *St. Catherine's Monastery, Sinai, Egypt: The Monastery that contains a Mosque*

(2) *Meryem Ana Evi (The House of the Virgin), Ephesus, Turkey, exterior*

(3) *Meryem Ana Evi (The House of the Virgin), Ephesus, Turkey, plan*

(4) *An armed Muslim guarding the entrance to the Church of the Holy Sepulcher, Jerusalem (detail from a 15th century miniature)*

(5) *The Muslim Saint Abu Walîd (c. 1086): a 13th century polychrome sculpture which stands on the right of the High Altar in Toledo Cathedral*

(6) *Mr. Nuseibeh: Muslim doorkeeper to the Church of the Holy Sepulcher*

(7) *Koranic verses on a column in Palermo Cathedral*

(8) *Polyglot inscription on a tomb in Palermo Cathedral*

(9) *The Church of Mary Magdalene and the Mosque of Omar, Jerusalem*

(10) *St. Francis and the Sultan (early miniature)*

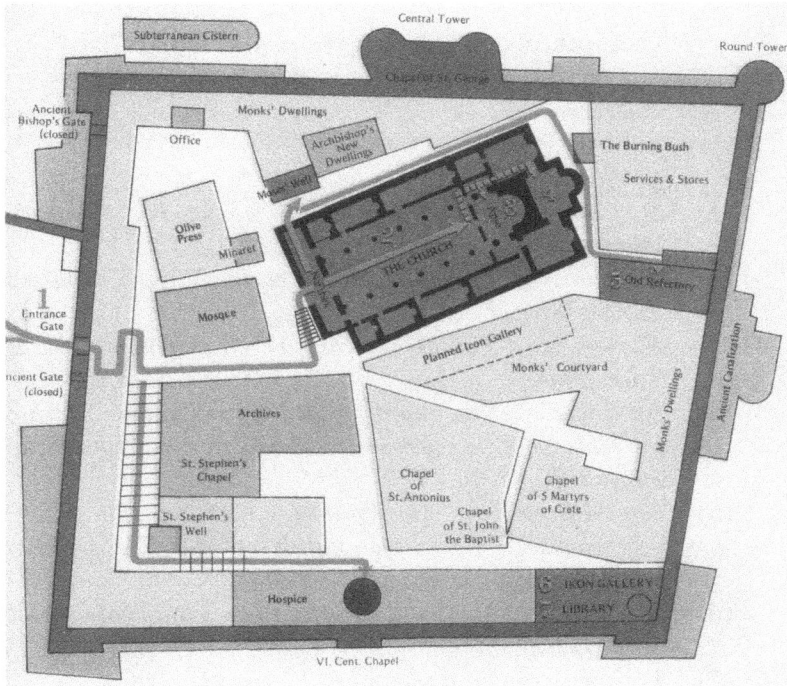

(1) St. Catherine's Monastery, Sinai, Egypt
(*The Monastery that contains a Mosque*)
(*See pp. 98-99*)

(2) *Meryem Ana Evi* (The House of the Virgin),
Ephesus, Turkey, exterior
(*See pp. 8-9*)

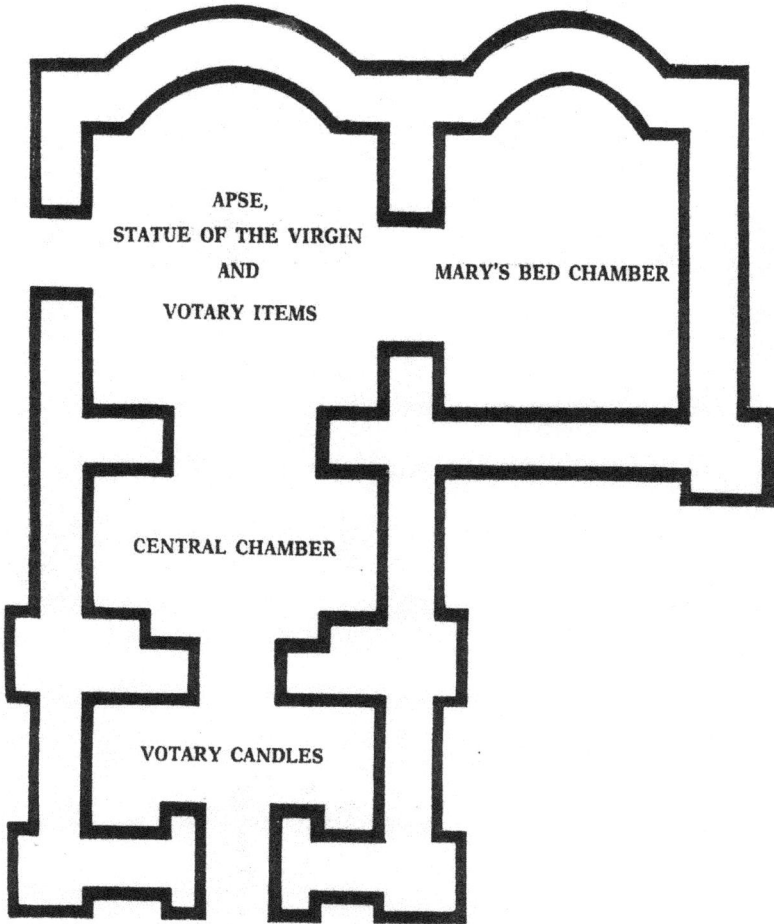

APSE,
STATUE OF THE VIRGIN
AND
VOTARY ITEMS

MARY'S BED CHAMBER

CENTRAL CHAMBER

VOTARY CANDLES

(3) *Meryem Ana Evi* (The House of the Virgin),
Ephesus, Turkey, plan
(*See pp. 8-9*)

**(4) An armed Muslim guarding the entrance to the
Church of the Holy Sepulcher, Jerusalem**
(*detail from a 15th century miniature*)

(5) A 13th century polychrome sculpture of the Muslim Saint Abu Walîd

(flourished in the late 11th century)
This statue was placed on the right-hand side of the
High Altar in Toledo Cathedral, Spain
two centuries after Abu Walîd's death,
and stands there to this day.
(See pp. 82-84)

(6) Mr. Nuseibeh: Muslim doorkeeper to the Church of the Holy Sepulcher

The function (keeper of the Key to the Church of the Holy Sepulcher, Jerusalem) has been in the hands of the Nuseibeh family for centuries. Their main job is to prevent the priests of the various Christian denominations from having fist-fights over the use of the building.

**(7) Koranic verses in Arabic on a column
in Palermo Cathedral, Sicily**
(See p. 34)

**(8) Inscription on the tombstone of
a Christian noblewoman (1148)
in the Cathedral of Palermo, Sicily**
(*See pp. 34-35*)

top:	Hebrew
bottom:	Arabic
left:	Latin
right:	Greek

*The four languages represent the four communities present in Sicily
during the Norman period (approx. 1070-1200)*

(9) The Church of Mary Magdalene and the Mosque of Omar,* Jerusalem

* This is generally know as *Qubbat as-Sahra*, "The Dome of the Rock". It is said that it was here that Abraham was ready to sacrifice his son, and also that it was the site from which the Prophet Mohammed ascended to Heaven.

(10) St. Francis and the Sultan (early miniature)
(*See p. 86*)

INDEX